Megan Daley is passionate about children's literature and sharing it with young and old alike. In daylight hours, Megan is a teacher librarian at a girls' school in Brisbane and was recently awarded the Queensland Teacher Librarian of the Year by the School Library Association of Queensland, as well as the national Dromkeen Librarian's Award, presented by the State Library of Victoria. A former national vice-president of the Children's Book Council of Australia, she is currently on the Queensland chapter of the board of the Australian Children's Laureate and is a judge for the Queensland Literary Awards. She blogs about all things literary, library and tech at childrensbooksdaily.com. She also thinks sleep is overrated.

raising readers

How to nurture a child's love of books

MEGAN DALEY

First published 2019 by University of Queensland Press
PO Box 6042, St Lucia, Queensland 4067 Australia
Reprinted 2019, 2022, 2023

uqp.com.au
reception@uqp.com.au

Cover design and illustration by Jo Hunt
Author photograph by Simone C Photography
Typeset in 11/16pt Legacy Serif by Jo Hunt
Printed in Australia by McPherson's Printing Group

University of Queensland Press is supported by the Queensland Government through Arts Queensland.

University of Queensland Press is assisted by the Australian Government through the Australia Council, its arts funding and advisory body.

A catalogue record for this book is available from the National Library of Australia.

ISBN 978 0 7022 6257 9 (pbk)
ISBN 978 0 7022 6361 3 (pdf)
ISBN 978 0 7022 6362 0 (epub)
ISBN 978 0 7022 6363 7 (kindle)

University of Queensland Press uses papers that are natural, renewable and recyclable products made from wood grown in well-managed forests and other controlled sources. The logging and manufacturing processes conform to the environmental regulations of the country of origin.

For our boys:

Daniel John Daley
AKA our Chief Bedtime Books Reader
10 August 1976 – 29 April 2017
Eternally reading Ranger's Apprentice by John Flanagan

Simon James Dean
5 September 1982 – 28 January 2012
Eternally reading *Looking for Trouble* by John Marsden

CONTENTS

INTRODUCTION

I have loved books my whole life. I was fortunate to be raised in a home that valued words and literature, and my parents read to me throughout my childhood and beyond. I vividly remember my father reading to me in my early teens; though, perhaps, he was reading to my younger brothers and I was just part of the action. Regardless, I was hooked by the sound of words being recited by someone I loved and admired. My mother, who was also a teacher librarian, filled our house with quality books. She introduced me to some of my all-time favourites, including *Dicey's Song* (Cynthia Voigt), *Came Back to Show You I Could Fly* (Robin Klein) and John Marsden's iconic *So Much to Tell You* – which blew my teenage angsty brain!

When I had my first child it came as something of a shock that others around me were not reading to their babies. And in my role at the time as national vice-president of the Children's Book Council of Australia, I was asked several times over by the media or parents about the 'right age' to start reading to children. The answer seemed obvious to me – from birth, of course! I would tell people that books were an essential newborn accessory. But I also had to be mindful that not everyone had my upbringing or training or knowledge of childhood literacy. On a personal level, fostering a love of reading in my children seemed to be the easiest part of parenting. I find being a parent a very hard job at times and every stage of child-rearing seems to be filled with guilt. I do, however, feel confident that I will be able to look back and say, 'But I read to them and gave them the joy of books' and know that I did my best.

I have been a teacher librarian for over fifteen years and a primary school teacher for twenty. As a parent and educator, I know how beneficial it is for children to enter the education system bubbling with excitement about words, images and ideas. Flashcards or early online reading programs won't instil this joy in your little one, but gorgeous books will. Immersing your child in language in all forms – stories and songs and nursery rhymes – is one of the best ways you can give them a head start and help them to reach their academic potential. We educators are always so grateful to the families who read to their children and support the education process in this way. It is possible to encourage the joy of recreational reading and still meet the demands of the school curriculum and data requirements, but families are crucial in helping us achieve this.

Raising Readers is a guide for parents and a resource for educators. Like all good non-fiction books (my teacher librarian hat is on now), you can dip into this book as needed or you can read it from start to finish. I will walk you through each stage of a child's literacy development – from birth to adolescence – and offer advice, connect you with the right books at the right times, share pieces of wisdom from my literary friends, as well as some tips and tricks to ensure your family's or classroom's reading journeys are as memorable and as engaging as they can be.

Throughout the book I refer to school libraries and library staff as if they exist in every school. I do this because they darned well should and the research supports this. I don't believe good school libraries and quality teacher librarians and library staff are a thing of the past, but if you are in a school without a library or teacher librarian, I hope that this book offers you guidance. We all have an invaluable part to play in ensuring the young people in our lives fall in love with books. It is a gift they will cherish forever.

CHAPTER ONE

RAISING A READER – THE EARLY YEARS

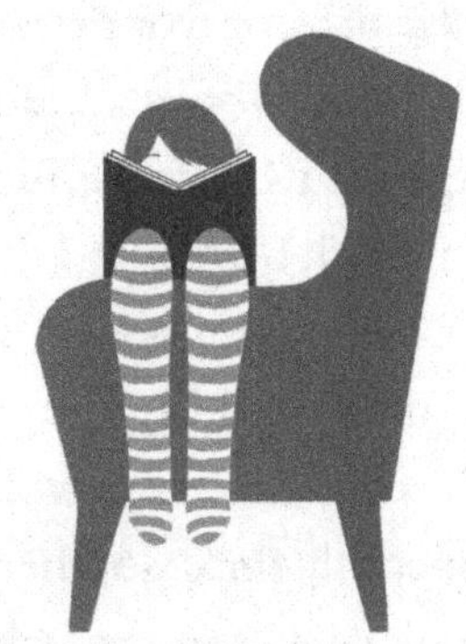

FROM BABIES TO TWO YEARS OLD

Babies will start to show interest in books much earlier than you might think. Shortly after birth, infants respond to sound, often turning towards it, and start focusing their vision. After three to four months of listening and looking at the world, many infants will begin to reach for objects.[1] As they gain control over their movements, babies will explore books in the same way they do a rattle or toy. They will chew them, turn them over and stare at them. They will be intrigued by bright, contrasting colours, and soothed by a calm voice reading a story or singing a song. For babies, hearing the rhythm of words and the expression in voices builds a rich and diverse network of language in their developing brains.

I read a large number of novels when I had newborns as I found myself sitting in chairs rocking or feeding the baby for many hours a day. I became adept at cradling my e-reader in one hand in exactly the right position – at this stage paper books didn't seem safe as I needed to use two hands and no one wants to drop a brick of a novel on their newborn! I mostly read my books aloud and while I'm sure the content was wildly inappropriate, I figured that my babies didn't understand the words. I did know, however, that they were hearing language that was far more complex and diverse than if I was just having a casual chat with them – though, of course, casual chats are also extremely important![2] Some parents may feel silly reading to their baby or wonder what the point is, but the key here is exposure. The more you read aloud to your child, the more words they'll be exposed to and the more solid their foundation for future literacy skills will be.

From around six months old, babies who have been read to regularly will begin to identify a book as more than just a colourful object – the book will signal that 'it's time for a story'. This is especially the case when parents or caregivers respond by reading the book whenever the baby hands one to them.[3] Babies may develop a liking for a particular book and frequently pick it up to be read, or become animated and excited when a favourite book is re-read.

Very early on, a baby develops literacy skills using all their senses, including touch. The sense of touch enables babies to attach meaning to objects, from cups and shoes to the pet dog and, of course, books. They explore the mechanics of how books work by turning pages and touching the covers and illustrations. Lift-the-flap and touch-and-feel titles are wonderful for babies and toddlers because they encourage physical engagement with books. Touch and physical contact are finely integrated in language development,[4] from the parent or carer cuddling the child when reading, to the child exploring the physical nature of a book, and then later, as early readers, when they trace words with their finger as they read text or manipulate digital texts on a tablet device. That's why it's important to have plenty of books around your house within easy access of your child – so that they have ample opportunities to hold, explore and play with books.

From around ten months old, babies may comprehend their first word, and by twelve months many will say their first word. Acquiring and comprehending words is a slow process until around eighteen months when many children become rapid word learners.[5]

Toddlers are little sponges, soaking up everything there is to learn. They adore words, nursery rhymes, songs and books. Of course, toddlers are also destructive little bunnies! Because they are still learning how a book works and because they use *all* their senses to 'read', chewing and ripping may occur! But do not let the possible destruction stop you from reading to them. This is the time to get your kids hooked on books.

For younger toddlers I think board books are a great option for unsupervised book time as they are relatively indestructible. However, the text in board books is often minimal, so they should not make up your entire collection for this age group. It's important to also introduce beautiful picture books rich in both language and artwork. Exposing little ones to gorgeous illustrations, exquisite writing and the joy of story is the best way to help them fall in love with books.

The social nature of reading comes into play around this time, as toddlers become aware of their peers and are able to engage in literacy opportunities in unstructured learning environments.[6] Toddlers in childcare or playgroups may use books in the same way they will use toys - one may show another how it works, there will be tussles over favourites and, *eventually*, there will be sharing and exchanging of books. When toddlers share a book they are supporting each other in their learning,[7] - for example, one child might name the animals in the illustrations and the other might make the sounds. In an early education centre, toddlers will often be observed reaching for a book that was previously shared by an educator. They may 're-read' the book for themselves and this independent and unstructured reading time is as meaningful as the group reading session; in fact, it is one of the earliest forms of literate behaviour.

Reading with babies and toddlers

Here are some tips to help make reading with your baby or toddler a fun experience for you both, the operative word being FUN!

- Choose a time when your baby is content and alert.
- Cuddle up with your child. Reading is the perfect time for physical bonding.
- Choose books with fabulous pictures and minimal but engaging text.
- Keep reading sessions short, snappy and regular. Don't feel like you have to finish the book. You might only get through a few pages at a time.
- Babies and toddlers love looking at pictures of themselves and their loved ones, so consider making a photo book – a lovely keepsake as well as a literacy tool.
- Feel free to bounce or tickle or rock your baby as you read – anything that makes reading fun. The same applies to toddlers. Allow them to wriggle and spin as you read. They are (mostly) not going to sit still for the length of a book.
- Moderate your voice and use expression to make the story come alive. Add in animal noises or other sound effects.
- Allow children to chew, touch and smell their books to get the sensory thing happening. Not ideal in an early education environment but totally okay at home!
- Be prepared to lose a book or two. When there are toddlers in the house, have a selection of books within their reach so they can instigate reading sessions, but keep your precious ones higher up for one-on-one reading time. That said, forget pop-up books for the time being. They'll be shredded in a nanosecond.
- Encourage interaction with the book. Ask questions like: 'Can you point to the horse?'; 'Where is that silly monkey hiding? Can you see him?'

- Show and encourage page turning.
- Be prepared to read books over and over again (endlessly!). It might drive you bonkers but babies and toddlers love repetition - it's how they learn.
- This tip doesn't involve a book per se, but songs and nursery rhymes are incredibly useful literacy tools, so sing to your child whenever you get the chance. It doesn't matter if you can't carry a tune in a bucket - your kids will love it!

THE IMPORTANCE OF SONG

Like reading, it is never too early to sing to a baby. Parents and caregivers will have experienced how effectively singing a song can calm a baby or entrance a toddler. Song is tightly intertwined with language development and, like books, no child should be without song in their life. Research has found that music is a powerful tool in language acquisition and that the processing of music and language occur in the same areas of the brain and share the same neural pathways.[8] I have been fortunate to work with some talented music educators, including Dr James Cuskelly, Carla Trott and Jennifer Teh. Jennifer Teh's music classes for babies and toddlers were an important part of our weekly routine for some time, and I have asked her to share her thoughts on the role of song in language development.

Jennifer Teh

Singing is an intrinsic part of raising children. When a baby cries, it feels right to hum a lullaby. We sing action songs and nursery rhymes with our toddlers and young children. Song is a unique way of connecting and communicating, and it carries with it benefits for both the singer and the listener.

Many wonderful things happen when a child is sung to. Songs can be used for storytelling, cultural exchange, to calm, to excite and to incite discussion. For the singer, the act of singing increases cardiovascular function, lowers blood pressure, releases endorphins and lowers stress levels, with consequent increase in immune function. Singing to babies is particularly powerful.. All positive mother–baby interaction leads to the release of beta endorphins for both, promoting feelings of wellbeing and increased relaxation, and this is especially true when a baby is being held and sung to.

There is a direct correlation between singing and the development of language. The folk songs of every culture carry with them the signature inflections of the 'mother tongue' language, and help to wire the child's ear, voice and brain to engage with this language. If you are worried that you don't sing well enough, relax! For your child, your voice is the safest and most familiar sound, and is far better than any recorded music. Just as children learn language in interactive environments by being engaged in live conversation, they will gain the most benefit from being sung to directly by their caregivers.

You can begin singing to your child before they are even born – amniotic fluid is a great conductor of sound. Babies begin to respond to sound in the womb from around eighteen weeks gestation, and the ability to recognise voices and even songs develops quite significantly by the end of pregnancy. All through my pregnancy with my son Joshua, my husband Jamie sang one song to my belly, over and over again. When Josh was born, Jamie held him and sang that song, and immediately Josh stopped crying and stared quietly at him (and our midwife started to cry instead). As an infant Josh would still settle immediately whenever Jamie sang 'You Are My Sunshine'.

Sometimes it is hard to know WHAT to sing to your child, but there are many fabulous books designed to be sung to children of all ages – from illustrated nursery rhymes, to sung stories like *The Wonky Donkey* by Craig Smith. Other books haven't necessarily been created with the purpose of being sung but seem to naturally lend themselves to it, for example, books written in rhyming verse. But you can sing to your child about everything and anything, so fill your day with music.

BOOKS FOR BABIES AND TODDLERS

All book recommendation lists in *Raising Readers* do not include well-known or classic books. I have instead selected less obvious choices and my personal favourites. Consider each list as a springboard for you to seek out other books that might be a good fit for your young reader.

Whoever You Are by Mem Fox, illustrated by Leslie Staub (Scholastic Australia, 2015)

Dreamers by Ezekiel Kwaymullina, illustrated by Sally Morgan (Fremantle Press, 2014)

At the Beach I See by Kamsani Bin Salleh (Magabala Books, 2017)

What the Sky Knows by Nike Bourke, illustrated by Stella Danalis (University of Queensland Press, 2005)

For All Creatures by Glenda Millard, illustrated by Rebecca Cool (Walker Books Australia, 2011)

Puffling by Margaret Wild, illustrated by Julie Vivas (Scholastic Australia, 2008)

Kissed by the Moon by Alison Lester (Penguin Books Australia, 2013)

Goodnight, Me by Andrew Daddo, illustrated by Emma Quay (Hachette Australia, 2005)

Birthday Baby by Davina Bell and Jane Godwin, illustrated by Freya Blackwood (Allen & Unwin, 2018)

Baby Band by Dianne Jackson Hill, illustrated by Giuseppe Poli (New Frontier Publishing, 2017)

Yoga Babies by Fearne Cotton, illustrated by Sheena Dempsey (New Frontier Publishing, 2018)

FROM THREE TO FIVE YEARS OLD

It is tempting as children enter the preschool phase to turn shared reading time into a 'meaningful learning experience' in the belief that a child needs to be 'prepared' to enter the school system. Media representations of parenting are often fear-based, with parents left feeling their child will be disadvantaged if they are not signed up to the latest flashcard system or early online reading program. Intensive early intervention may produce a child who enters the school system seemingly 'reading' at a higher level, but as their peers learn to read at their own pace and 'catch up', those children with the *experience* of books, rather than those who have learnt sounds and words by rote, are often the ones with higher all-round reading comprehension and engagement with books. By all means, sing alphabet songs with your preschooler, practise recognising letters and sounds in words, and encourage them to write their name, but I urge parents and caregivers to keep it playful and be led by your child's interest and enthusiasm. Reading books is still the single most important activity you can do with your child in developing their literacy.

Young children respond with enthusiasm when books are presented in multiple forms or modalities. For example, bring a book to life with props such as puppets, weave in songs, ask children to act out scenes from a story, or get them involved in a hands-on way with felt books. Engaging all of your child's senses in book-based experiences is crucial in maintaining their attention and creating a sense of playfulness.

Technology gives us further opportunities to re-imagine contemporary reading practices. Preschoolers experience story in a different, yet interactive way when they engage with digital texts on touch-based devices. I will never forget when my then three-year-old swiped the paper page of *The Very Cranky Bear* in total frustration, trying to make the bear move. I was horrified yet fascinated that she hoped for 'more' from the paper book. I don't believe the print book will be replaced anytime soon, but it is a fact that print and digital stories share space on the bookshelf.

Children in this age group also often enjoy creating handmade books. Asking your child to tell you the 'story' of their picture and writing this down on the page helps young children make connections between images and words. They will also delight in using their little books to retell their story to a loved adult. This retelling of a story over and over is important in developing the idea of how a narrative works as well as the knowledge that words always stay the same on the page – that the letters d-o-g will always spell 'dog'. It is an absolute lightbulb moment when a child realises that text, those squiggles on a page, hold meaning, and writing and telling stories together is the perfect way to help your child make this discovery for themselves.

Reading with three- to five-year-olds

Although children in this age group generally have longer attention spans, they are still easily distracted by food, an adored older sibling or any bright shiny object! So keep book time fun to keep young readers interested. Here are a few tactics I have used with my own young children and in early education centres.

- Turn off the TV and put away the iPad. It can be hard to focus on a book when there are colourful, bright images constantly flashing by!
- Kids love humour so put on funny voices or make sound effects to keep them engaged. Used sparingly, audio books can be a perfect addition for children around this age. They will love the variety in voices and start to understand how tone, pitch and pace can alter the feel of a story.
- Be interactive. Talk about what's happening in the story; ask your child to guess what's going to happen next; point out interesting details in the illustrations.

- Act out or add actions to parts of the story, or ask your child to do so. If you're not confident in this, try using props such as toys or puppets. Some books even come with finger puppets included as part of a pack.
- Talk about the parts of a book and physically point to the cover, pages, text, images and the spine.
- Follow the text with your finger so your child can see the way words flow from left to right.
- Be prepared to re-read favourite books over and over again. I promise they will one day move on to another book – although my now seven-year-old still makes me occasionally re-read her favourite dinosaur book from when she was two, and I suspect she will be requesting this book into her teen years!
- Tell your kids how much you love reading with them. The emotional bond children form with books, through a loved adult enjoying the process with them and articulating this enjoyment, should not be underestimated.

ESTABLISHING READING ROUTINES

Establishing a reading routine from a young age helps children to develop strong lifelong reading habits. A child's love of books begins with loved adults taking the time out from a busy schedule to read with them. It's a wonderful bonding exercise. Cuddling up and reading with a child allows them to form powerful associations between books and moments of happiness, love and closeness.

But life can be stressful and it can be difficult to keep reading at the top of the priority list when there are work crises to deal with, children to wrangle, bills to pay, and so on. Every family has their own set of challenging circumstances. Making reading part of the daily routine helps to ensure that it happens because it becomes

BOOKS FOR THREE- TO FIVE-YEAR OLDS

I don't believe you ever grow out of picture books. Though my children are no longer preschoolers, I will be keeping the books on this list forever. We have created special memories by reading these books together and so they have become treasured possessions.

The Last Peach by Gus Gordon (Penguin Books Australia, 2018)

Tom Tom by Rosemary Sullivan, illustrated by Dee Huxley (HarperCollins, 2010)

Monster Party by the children of the Rawa Community School, with Jane Godwin and Alison Lester (Magabala Books, 2018)

My Dog Bigsy by Alison Lester (Penguin Books Australia, 2015)

Cheeky Monkey by Andrew Daddo, illustrated by Emma Quay (ABC Books, 2010)

It's Bedtime, William by Deborah Niland (Penguin Books Australia, 2012)

The Game of Finger Worms by Hervé Tullet (Phaidon Press Ltd, 2011)

Watch This! A Book About Making Shapes by Jane Godwin, Beci Orpin and Hilary Walker (Scribble, 2018)

I'm a Hungry Dinosaur by Janeen Brian and Ann James (Penguin Books Australia, 2015)

I Do Not Like Books Anymore! by Daisy Hirst (Walker Books, 2018)

Rock Pool Secrets by Narelle Oliver (Walker Books Australia, 2017)

Do Not Lick This Book by Idan Ben-Barak and Julian Frost (Allen & Unwin, 2017)

All the Ways to be Smart by Davina Bell, illustrated by Allison Colpoys (Scribble, 2018)

The Cleo Stories series by Libby Gleeson, illustrated by Freya Blackwood (Murdoch Books, 2014)

This is a Ball (and others in series) by Beck Stanton and Matt Stanton (ABC Books, 2015) automatic, like brushing your teeth or turning on the dishwasher. But it also means that you're consistently carving out moments for yourself to relax and relish dedicated time with your child.

Bedtime reading is often the easiest routine to put in place as it is already a time of calmness, closeness and winding down from a busy day (more on this soon). However, there may be other opportunities throughout your day where reading routines can be established. There's no right or wrong time. Do whatever will work best for you and your family.

Going to the free 'Rhyme Time' or 'Babies and Books' sessions at your local library is a great way to incorporate fun literacy activities into your schedule. As I've mentioned, songs and nursery rhymes are wonderful tools for a child's language development. But 'Rhyme Time' or 'Babies and Books' sessions have the added benefit of filling your little one with the joyful feelings that come from being in a social setting.

Visiting the local library to sign my newborn up for a library card was one of the first outings I had with both my children. For many years, my friends and I were in a weekly routine of meeting at the public library for nursery rhyme, music and storytelling sessions with our young babies. Our goal was to expose our children to the sights and sounds of language, but it also became a time for us to discuss, debate and recommend baby books (and some adult ones for ourselves!), leave with armfuls of library loans, and connect with like-minded parents over the trials and tribulations of raising small children.

Bedtime reading

In our house, my husband, Dan, was the chief bedtime book reader for many years until his death. At one point the Daddy bedtime books routine was a complicated and strict ritual involving two books, a thumb wrestle, two squashy hugs and something else

I don't remember. It was lovely hearing Dan and our girls laugh over funny stories or argue about re-reading a book for the fifth night in a row. I am so pleased my children had these early years with a father who read to them, and I suspect this will be a treasured memory they carry into adulthood.

Bedtime reading is definitely a routine worth aiming for. Sometimes, when I am exhausted by solo parenting or when the end of school term is nigh and I'm surrounded by small cranky people, it is so tempting to skip the bedtime books. But when I reflect on the benefits of a bedtime reading routine in my own life, it's clear to me why I make the effort nearly every night to do it.

- Bedtime books make me *stop*. I am on full throttle. All the time. I sleep very little and I never sit still, but reading bedtime books makes me hit the pause button. Almost instantly I feel my frenetic energy dissipate.
- I have to be present and mindful to read. I can't be on my phone, I can't be washing or working. I have to read the words and engage with the story. I am entirely present with my children and the book we are reading together. For more on mindful reading see chapter 12.
- No matter how chaotic and *loud* and plain horrid the evening has been, bedtime reading is a change of focus and completely resets the mood in the house.
- It (almost) always happens. The routine makes me feel like everything will be okay, like I've *got* this parenting thing. Mostly.
- Books spark conversations. Every afternoon I ask my girls, 'What did you do today?' and *every* day I get nothing. But later that night we might read a book about friends or feelings, and they suddenly start talking about their day at school or an issue with a friend. When my daughters see their lives reflected in the pages of book, talk happens.

- Going to sleep with dreams of fairies, dinosaurs or adventures is far better than dreams of being yelled at to floss your teeth properly. It's the last thing you do at night with your children, so make it wonderful.

Despite my lifelong love of books, some nights it is just too much, and I tell my children to read alone or I put on an audio story or streamed reading service like Story Box Library – perfectly acceptable alternatives and no guilt needed! However, I can see the benefits, for *myself* as well as my girls, so I try really hard, take a deep breath and squash into a single bed with them, hoping the youngest doesn't sink her teeth into her sister to make her move over. And then we read.

Even if it is only for fifteen minutes, that time spent reading is precious. Being physically close, squished up together, and escaping into an imaginary world through books reduces my stress and anxiety like nothing else I know. Whether you are a single parent, have multiple children or you work long hours, bedtime reading may be the one time in the day when you are completely present with your family. I never regret those fifteen minutes (which often turn into thirty). It's like exercise – you always feel better once you start, or so I'm told.

Challenges to bedtime reading

Time poor: Work on enlisting the help of other loved adults in your child's life, such as neighbours, grandparents or older siblings. For example, if your child has long-distance grandparents, perhaps they could share a book together over the phone or handheld tablet.

Reluctant readers: The thought of an argument just before sleeping time may be enough to prevent a parent from attempting bedtime books with their reluctant reader. The thing to remember is that for a reluctant reader, one-on-one book time with a loved adult can ignite the spark for a love of reading or at least a love of story. My advice here is simple – persist, persist, persist. Even when you feel like you are getting nowhere it is worth it, I promise. Choosing books that have a connection with a particular person is a good strategy here. Maybe Nonna always reads *My Nanna is a Ninja* (Damon Young and Peter Carnavas) so it becomes 'her' book, or you might have a football-loving family member for whom *Why I Love Footy* (Michael Wagner and Tom Jellett) is exclusively reserved.

Choosing the book: Dear glory, the battles we have in our house! We take it in turns, myself included, and we switch it up. Some weeks we will read picture books. Then we might spend a week on puzzle books and then we might have two weeks of reading a longer chapter book. Some people would suggest that the child should choose the bedtime books; but I, with my educator hat on, would argue that bedtime reading is the perfect time to introduce a new genre, explore a book at a higher literacy level, or share one of your own beloved novels from childhood. Taking it in turns means that everyone has choice, but there is also balance, compromise and a variety of reading material.

If you are passionate about literacy and can see the benefits offered by regular bedtime (or other time) books, consider becoming involved with The Pyjama Foundation, which currently operates throughout Queensland, New South Wales and Victoria. Bronwyn Sheehan founded the organisation in 2004 because she wanted *more* for children living in foster care: more hope, more opportunities and more books in their lives. The Pyjama Foundation trains volunteers called Pyjama Angels, who are matched with a child in care. They spend an hour a week with that one child reading books, playing educational games and helping with homework. The work of The Pyjama Foundation is so important in offering a more positive outlook for children in care. For more information see **www.thepyjamafoundation.com**.

INCIDENTAL READING

Fitness experts talk about the importance of incidental exercise, so surely a teacher librarian can talk about incidental reading?! Incidental reading is all about snatching pockets of time in a busy day to quickly escape into a book with your child. It could be while you're waiting for the bath to fill or while you're killing time before a doctor's appointment. The key to incidental reading is to surround yourself with books so that they can be easily and regularly dipped into.

Place collections of books in baskets or boxes throughout your home, chuck a few board books in the nappy bag, and stash a few in the car. Around the time she was five, my daughter, whom I'll call PudStar (as I do online), decorated an empty shoebox and filled it with board books for her younger sister, ChickPea (another pseudonym from my blog). She asked me to write 'Car Library' on it. We used that box until it fell apart and have had many more 'Mobile Library' boxes since.

I often keep borrowed library books on the back seat, mostly so they don't get lost at home (which happens regularly, despite me being a librarian!). But having books in the car has also been a lifesaver for me. It doesn't always happen, but sometimes I can go on a 30-minute car trip with my girls not whingeing, fighting or constantly asking, 'Are we there yet?' It is such a simple thing to do and can work wonders.

It's incredibly easy to model reading as a necessary part of everyday life when you are out and about. Read road signs and menus aloud, or hand your child a catalogue in the supermarket and ask them to read or name the pictures of the items, and then have them add up two or three of them for some numeracy practice.

Five easy 'coffee shop packs' for incidental reading

I'm more than guilty of the 'here kids, have my phone while I drink my coffee' trick. No one wants to be the parent with the screaming children disturbing the entire café! But I also always carry books in my bag. For 'on the go' reading, I like to choose books that can be easily dipped in and out of, like a joke book or poetry anthology or fact book. I also keep 'coffee shop packs' – small bags or zippered folders with a book, pencil, paper and props – in the car. I like to have a number of different packs on rotation so that they retain their novelty value and my kids will stay interested in them. Here are my top five suggestions for easy 'coffee shop packs'.

1. Mini editions of children's books. These are often sold in school book club catalogues or around Christmas time as gift sets with soft toy characters. When she was young and compliant, my eldest child, PudStar, would neatly line up her five mini Olivia the Pig (Ian Falconer) books, decide which one to 'read', then settle down to look at the pictures and tell the stories to herself or her mini Olivia the Pig finger puppet. Her ability to independently immerse herself in this imaginary world was due, in part, to my mum having read these books endlessly to her. PudStar deeply absorbed the stories, which then informed her play.

2. Doodle books, colouring books and activity books. Doodle books are fab. They show a picture idea and the child is encouraged to continue drawing from it. For example, there might be an outline of a TV screen and the child can draw a scene within it. Just remember to include colouring pencils in the pack. Books of mazes, word games or quizzes are also great for older children.

3. A few nice picture books that are 'new' to the child. These might be library books or ones you rotate from home, but the important thing is that they are a bit of a novelty for the child.

4. 'Spot the difference' or other 'finding' books. These provide hours of entertainment as kids try to find small hidden things. I've set up the idea that my daughters have to find Wally all by themselves (mainly as I cannot stand these sorts of books).

5. Story stones. These are smooth pebbles with stickers or small paintings of characters, settings and objects, which can be used to tell stories. There are plenty of ideas online for making these yourself or, if craft glue is your kryptonite, you can also buy pre-made ones. At some stage I must have found it quite therapeutic to make these (cut, glue, repeat) as I had about twenty little drawstring bags of different sets of story stones, as well as some with sight words.

PLAYFUL READING

My favourite memories of my own childhood are of playing with my huge circle of family friends. Playing was just what we did – it was an organic part of our lives. Our parents never agonised over our choices of games or thought about creating 'meaningful learning experiences'. In those days, everyone seemed to accept that free play was a natural and essential part of childhood.

But of course we *were* learning through our play, as we constructed cubbyhouses and imaginary worlds; experimented with floating and sinking (the caterpillar didn't float – sorry, caterpillar); negotiated with our peers over what games to play next and who was 'it'; practised our numbers while baking and selling mud pies, and empathised with one another as bones were snapped on netless trampolines of the 1980s.

But these days, between technology, work, school and extracurricular activities, and the feeling that we must 'entertain and educate' our children at all times, free play seems to have fallen by the wayside. I cannot stress enough how play and literacy development go hand-in-hand. A game of 'shop' may require children to write and read shopping lists or food labels. A game of 'school' will often involve the 'teacher' asking the 'student' to write their own name or listen to a 'modelled book reading'. It is well documented in early literacy development research that parents and educators need to value play as an important and valid part in literacy development as children engage with and respond to stories, create their own stories, and learn about themselves and their world.[9]

Emma Schafer is a kindergarten teacher and advocate for literacy development through play-based learning experiences. Her learning spaces always have books dispersed throughout as well as a book corner or nook which offers children a place to escape the busyness of the classroom, a way to settle into their day, or a space to be immersed in story and imaginary worlds. Emma shares her thoughts below on playful reading in the kindergarten setting.

Emma Schafer

Play is an all-important, and sadly sometimes overlooked, aspect of child development. Play allows children to master social, emotional and academic skills while interacting with peers and the world around them. The mastery of social skills through play develops resilience, problem-solving, empathy and kindness. Through play, children learn to work alongside and with each other, negotiate roles and problem solve conflicts. They practise their decision-making skills, act out and work through scenarios and interact with a diverse range of peers and adults in a safe environment.

Quality literature and picture books play a pivotal role in play-based learning and language acquisition. Children most often role-play situations that they know and understand. Most preschools, kindergartens and prep rooms will have a home corner where you will see children playing various family games. Children take on the roles that they are most familiar with, act them out and make up variations on these games – often informed by the books we have been reading. In doing so, children are developing an understanding of how different roles in the world work, how different families operate, and are challenged by other children when something doesn't go as planned. Role-play in the early years is a way for children to 'try out' the lives of others, such as being a parent and looking after the crying babies (you wouldn't believe how unsettled the 'babies' in my classroom are).

Picture books give young children the visuals for the words on the page. They form an important part of our daily routine and are embedded into our program to support, inform and extend children's play. We read a wide range of books based on the children's interests and every year we find that different groups of children take different things out of the same books.

As a kindergarten teacher I have the luxury of following the children's interests and designing areas in the classroom to further support these interests. I also have books in outdoor spaces where much play occurs – yes, these books will not last as long, but they are an important component in our play spaces. We often add things to our home corner or change it up completely based on the children's interests, which very often stem from a book we have read. I place high value on books and I model this through the way I respect and engage with books. We read every day and children frequently bring in their favourite book from home. These books are carefully placed on the whiteboard each morning, ready to be shared, discussed and enjoyed together. I find that there is often a trend with books that come in from home, demonstrating that children make connections with books we read at kindergarten and similar books they have at home. We may get a run on animal books or books about school or even books by the same author.

Recently we read a Hairy Maclary book in class and the children loved the predictability of the text with the rhyming dog names and were able to playfully join in the reading experience. This one book resulted in an influx of Hairy Maclary books from home to share with the class. A group of children were enjoying pretending to be dogs and role-playing with their peers. This play was completely organic, and in our classroom we encourage the children to ask their educators for extra props if they required. This led to quite a detailed discussion about what they needed for their 'doggie' play. We ended up making a variety of tails, which have been ever so popular, and this imaginative play continued for a couple of weeks. It encouraged children to use verbal and non-verbal language, take turns, share both resources and the different roles they had created within their game, and let us not forget the gross motor skills these children developed when crawling around the classroom!

I almost always use books as the starting point for new topics of interest. A recent unit of work on fairytales involved a huge number of books. Each fairytale was read to the children and they re-enacted the stories incidentally in their play and explicitly through intentional teaching. The language opportunities, storytelling and retelling that flowed from this unit was a delight to witness. We always have a 'small world' area set up in our classroom where children are able to take a set of imaginative play objects and play with them whenever it suits their rhythm. This area is resourced with puppets, objects and props, and during our fairytale unit our small world space became larger than life! Houses were constructed for the Three Little Pigs and puppets were sourced or made to play Little Red Riding Hood and her grandmother.

Some of the children asked if they could act out some of the stories with an audience, so we created a stage and seating; there were even tickets to the show. This simple example of a common unit or area of interest for kindergarten-age children demonstrates the power of books as a starting point for play, acquisition of literacy skills and engagement in the arts.

In a technology-filled and busy world with so many structured activities aimed at engaging young children and their parents, there is something refreshing and comforting about seeing young children playing organically, in their own time, following their own rhythm. Add books into the mix, and the power of the written word and beauty of the illustrations will take children's play to an even richer and more valuable place.

CHAPTER TWO

READING AND SCHOOL – WHEN IT ALL COMES TOGETHER

THE MECHANICS OF READING – WHERE TO BEGIN?

If I have noticed one thing from watching my children learn to read it's that reading will happen in its own time, so long as there are no identified literacy issues (see chapter 6 for more information). As a teacher I already knew this was the case, but when I became a parent, panic set in, as it does, and I spent much time crafting letter recognition and sight word games instead of just enjoying books with my girls. Maybe the sight word games helped, but I think what turned my children into 'readers' was surrounding them with beautiful words and images in picture books, and plenty of music.

My husband, Dan, and I also modelled a love of reading. I remember PudStar's brilliant prep teacher telling me that Pud had a great vocabularly around books – she talked about authors and illustrators all the time, and she knew what genres she liked and didn't like. Do not be discouraged if I have just described your home and yet you still have a child who is not 'a reader'. You can have the same recipe and the same family and yet one child will avidly read while the other two seem to do anything to avoid it; a few examples of this existed in my own childhood home! It is not an exact science, but I urge you to not decide too early that you have a 'non-reader'. Their time may just come - my youngest brother is now a voracious reader despite completely avoiding books as a child. Keep the structures in place, the modelled reading at a high level and the books strewn on every available surface, ready and waiting.

PHONICS AND SIGHT WORDS

I'm sure a few of us have experienced this scenario: child goes to first ever day of school pumped. Child comes home from first ever day of school sweaty, deflated and cranky, moaning, 'But I didn't learn how to read!'

Learning to read and becoming an independent reader is a process of incremental skill building. The first few years of primary school can seem to be a never-ending slog through sight words and frantic morning searches for those flimsy little school readers that teachers hand out daily with the reverence of a first edition Harry Potter. Those home readers often look like they have been through a washing machine or perhaps *need* to go through a washing machine, to remove the unidentifiable sticky residue on the cover. They appear lightweight in content and not particularly inspiring; yet teachers put great value on them, and on reading practice, so diligent parents play sight word games and churn through readers night after night.

There is a method in all of this and passionate teachers work tirelessly with their students in the teaching of this thing called phonics. Phonics is the teaching of letter-sound relationships. It is the understanding that there is a predictable relationship between the *sounds* of letters/letter combinations and the *look* of printed letters/letter combinations. The individual sound of a letter or letters ('th', 'igh', 'ough') is called a 'phoneme', and the letters that represent those sounds are called 'graphemes'.

When teaching phonics, teachers may use any number of programs and there are debates over which one is the most effective. Basically, most programs use a combination of explicit and sequential teaching of skills, and incidental teaching through the reading of books and environmental texts. Whatever the method, the desire of the teacher is the same: to build up strong neural pathways in children regarding the sound and sight of letters and letter combinations.

Alongside this alphabetic knowledge, sight words are introduced. Sight words are those words that cannot be decoded using the sight/sound approach. Lists of these words come home in the early years of school and give children the opportunity to build up a bank of high-frequency words and an understanding that not all words can be decoded (although there are various schools of thought on this and it is an ongoing educational debate).

Without knowledge of the alphabet, the letters and the sounds, as well as the blends that those sounds make, reading is impossible. Remembering words by sight will only get a young reader so far – soon enough they will need some strategies to decode unknown words. This is why sight words and phonics instruction are taught together.

Phonics lessons occur in all levels of primary school education but are at their most focused in the early years of primary school, with trained early childhood teachers being the experts in phonics instruction. As children move through to the middle years of primary school we talk more of spelling instruction, morphological elements like Greek and Latin roots and structural analysis of words.

Phonics is just one of many strategies used to teach reading and it should be handled with care and used sparingly. It is very easy to assume that teaching a child to read is merely a matter of practice, persistence and focus on accuracy, but these things are just part of the mix. The very best teachers plan for the reading needs and interests of their students, constantly monitor their progress and adjust teaching methods to support and extend as needed.

For suggestions on how to engage in collaborative play with sight words at home or in your early education setting, see 'How to play with sight words' (page 207). The emphasis should be on learning through collaborative play and shared discovery – a mix of incidental and planned activities is ideal.

READING COMPREHENSION

I am a passionate advocate of young people reading for pleasure. Reading is a chance for some downtime, and being motivated to read and being enthusiastic about reading has also been shown to have an important influence on the development of students' comprehension.[1] As young children decode words and sentences, they learn to construct meaning from a text by developing skills, making inferences, verifying understandings and making repairs to their reading.[2] Talking about books is one of the earliest ways in which parents and educators can engage a child in reading and encourage their comprehension of what has been read. Reading with young children should not always be a formal learning experience; however, it is great to get into the habit of creating dialogue around literature by asking questions and having informal discussions about the content, context or connections you have or can make with a book.

I've had excellent book conversations with toddlers and they relish the opportunity to chat with a trusted adult about a story they have enjoyed. With slightly older children who are just starting their 'learning to read' journey, it is really important to continue these book conversations. When your child starts to decipher words in a text, we adults can get so caught up in the excitement of this that we momentarily forget that comprehension is an essential element in the 'learning to read' process. I see plenty of very young children who are capable of reading the words but if you ask them a few questions about the content of the book, they are at a loss; their deep understanding of a book is not at the same skill level as their ability to decode words. Comprehension is central to reading development.

The following questions or conversation starters can be used with toddlers right through to independent readers. Modify as needed and add your own questions into the mix. Asking a question or two without making it a chore gives you an insight into your child's level of comprehension and encourages them to be critical readers of text.

The idea is not to work through this list of questions after each book is read – that is so not fun. If your child is in the mood, just casually ask one or two questions. To make this activity playful, I have written questions on paddle-pop sticks and put them in a bottle and turned it into a lucky dip game. Another suggestion is to make paper chatterboxes where your young reader can pick the question. Get creative and make up board games, or cardboard dice with questions written on them. There are no rules and you know your own children. The following questions will get the dice rolling (so to speak).

Reading comprehension question ideas

- Can you find the author's name on the cover?
- Can you find the illustrator's name?
- What do you think of the illustrations in the book? Are they painted? Drawn? Is it a collage? Photographs? Are they black and white or coloured? How is colour used?
- Which is your favourite illustration? Why? Can you describe the illustration?

- What do you think might happen next in the story?
- If you were the author of the story would you have finished it the same way?
- What did you like or dislike about this book?
- What do you think the author was trying to say to us? What helped you figure out the message?
- What part of the story was the most exciting or interesting?
- Which character was your favourite? Why?
- Did any of the characters remind you of anyone you know?
- Can you think of any other books that are similar to this one?
- Look at the cover. Did it give you clues about the story?
- Point to the parts of the book when I call them out: spine, front cover, back cover, blurb, title.
- How did this book make you feel? Was it a happy book? Thoughtful? A bit scary? An adventure?
- What would be a good food to eat while reading this book?
- What is the setting of this story?
- Can you ask *me* a question about the book we just read?
- Can you retell the story?
- Who is telling the story?
- Can you think of a friend who might also like this book? Why do you think they would like it?

Another strategy to increase discussion about books and the way they work is to search out books that are about books. I have two favourites – *Parsley Rabbit's Book about Books* (Frances Watts and David Legge) and *Lucy's Book* (Natalie Jane Prior and Cheryl Orsini). Full disclosure: I am the image of the librarian in *Lucy's Book*. Even after ten years I am still very fond of *Parsley Rabbit* and regularly use it in library lessons. Written for an early childhood audience, Parsley Rabbit walks us through a book that is all about books and along the way he points out the title, endpapers, spine, the way the words move from left to right on a page, and the many more parts and workings of a book. Utterly brilliant. *Lucy's Book* introduces young readers from early childhood to middle primary to the concept of libraries but also the idea that a book can be loved by many and is a resource to be shared. Even if I were not pictured in this book (complete with pink hair and some of my favourite clothes!), this would be the best book I have found that captures the essence of libraries and love for a special book.

READERS VERSUS LIBRARY BOOKS

I often have parents visit my school library early in the year to find books that their child will be able to read by themselves. I relish the opportunity to launch into my spiel about the difference between 'learn to read' books (teacher-chosen levelled readers) and recreational books (self-selected library books). Term One of the first year of school is completely overwhelming for students, staff and parents, and each year I think that I would dearly love to sit 'new to the school system' parents down with a cup of tea and possibly some Persian love cake spiced with saffron, rose, cardamom and lemon (I digress), and talk them through the differences between classroom readers and recreational reads. Instead, while I have you here, make yourself a tea, grab a slice of cake and settle in.

Once phonics instruction is underway and parents are having endless 'fun, fun, fun for everyone' with sight word games, the next level of reading instruction is added to the homework folder - the home reader. Readers are short texts, specifically designed for the purpose of teaching reading.

To the capable adult reader they may appear dull and

uninteresting, but to the child learning to read they are just about the most wonderful thing in the world. Classroom readers are designed as teaching tools, with high-frequency sight words, simple sentences, predictable storylines, pictures which help to decode the text and a levelled system where books increase in difficulty as reading mastery is achieved. It is widely accepted that the early years of reading instruction are crucial in developing proficient readers, and classroom readers form part of the 'learn to read toolkit', alongside a suite of other strategies and ongoing monitoring of student progress.[3]

By week two of term the library lessons start, and library bags full of big picture books are dragged home like treasure sacks. The sheer volume of texts coming through your house in those early primary schools years can be *overwhelming*. Even I, a teacher librarian, find the number of library books formidable at times.

Books borrowed from libraries are self-selected, recreational reads and help young people develop an emotional attachment to reading and develop lifelong reading habits. Picture books and early chapter books are complex interplays between words and text, and require young people to think deeply, imagine, wonder and interpret. They contain sophisticated language that requires discussion and increases your child's vocabulary. They are also full of images that add to and extend the text.

Young people need both classroom readers and recreational reads – each supports the other and each has a distinct purpose. Classroom readers are great for using as part of your child's homework routine, where a parent or caregiver can support the reader in feeling a sense of accomplishment as they decode words and make meaning from a text. They are used in the classroom context to teach specific skills, to model writing styles, and to test reading ability. Teachers will have a goal in mind for each child: lower level readers help to develop confidence and fluency, while higher level readers extend and challenge – both are of critical importance in helping children become independent readers. Quality early childhood teachers are to be trusted; they are experts in what each students needs in a school or home reader. So don't change your child's reader level without first discussing your concerns with the teacher.

Books that your child has chosen from the library are for sharing with a loved adult and are usually a read-aloud experience until your child is reading independently. Even then, reading aloud is something which I encourage well into the upper primary years and beyond.

Focusing on developing a sense of joy around reading, rather than on what level your child is reading and where their peers are at, is so very important. Over-focusing on home readers and turning them into a battle can turn a love of reading into an intense dislike, as perfectly captured in the gorgeous picture book *I Do Not Like Books Anymore!* (Daisy Hirst). Unless there are diagnosed literacy issues, all children will learn to read at some point, but the journey often determines the strength of the outcome and those children who associate books with joy will always come out on top.

Award-winning children's author Pamela Rushby can write the most insanely beautiful prose, but often I find her name on a very 'constrained' levelled reader. I asked her about why and how she writes in these vastly different ways.

Pamela Rushby

I've been writing for both trade and educational publishers for more than twenty years and in that time I've had over 200 educational books published. Which sounds impressive until you remember that some of these books are only about eight pages long, and might contain only twenty (or fewer) words. These, believe it or not, are the hardest ones of all to write.

Trade books are the ones you'll find in bookshops, as well as public and school libraries. They're recreational reading: books you choose and love to read. Educational books are largely found in classrooms.

If you looked at a number of trade books and educational books lined up on a shelf, you might not be able to see much of a difference between them. They're all attractive to children, they're entertaining, they're colourful, they're well edited, they're well illustrated. But there is a difference. Educational books are carefully designed, by educational experts, to give children in classrooms practice in reading, to introduce them to new ideas and concepts, to develop reading skills, to build confidence, and to put children's learning into a broad context.

For a writer, choosing to write for the educational market is a whole different ballgame to choosing to write for trade.

A friend of mine once said that a writer's brain is like a lava lamp. At the bottom there's a whole gooey, pulsating mass of thoughts and ideas. Every once in a while, one idea might go *bloop!* and rise to the top. You'll think about it for a while, it'll change shape, perhaps get bigger, another idea might join onto it. Then it'll sink to the bottom again. But one day, that idea will rise to the top and won't go away, and you'll think, *Aha! There's a story!*

That's the way it works when I write for the trade market. I start out with an idea I've had. It's been blooping around in the lava lamp for quite a while, growing and developing. When it's ready to go, I'll know, because it just won't go away. And soon I'll be writing that story, because I desperately want to write it. (And fingers crossed a publisher will, eventually, want it too.)

When I write for the educational market I'm almost always writing commissioned material. A publisher has decided to produce a new series of books and invited writers to contribute to the series. The publisher will have an absolutely clear idea of what the series is intending to achieve, and the writer will receive a brief that outlines the publisher's needs and expectations. Let me give you an example.

A brief I received for some beginner reading books asked me to write a story about 'weather and its effect on people'. I had 120 to 150 words to do this. I needed to include certain high-frequency words at least eight times in the text. I also needed to include a phonic element and/or a vocabulary element from a given list. Oh, and it would be nice, the brief concluded, if I could manage to be funny, too.

Quite a challenge.

After a lot of thought and juggling of ideas and words (and a certain amount of whingeing, whining and despair), it was possible. I did it.

The trick is to approach a brief as if it's a puzzle to be solved. It may take some time, but, like a cryptic crossword, it can be done. It's a totally different way of writing from coming up with your own idea and developing your own story exactly as you want it to be.

One of the misconceptions people have about educational books is that they're boring. Well, in the past some certainly were. You may have memories of some of them. (*See Spot run. Run, Spot, run.*) But writers now see it as a challenge to make the books fun as well as meeting their educational aims. The one I'm working on features Spacegirl, a superhero who saves the universe by lassoing planets. I'm restricted to a very limited vocabulary and word count, (similar to the See Spot Run books), but I'm having fun with it – and I hope the kids will enjoy them too.

Usually editors from the publishing house will provide suggested topics to write about, although I've found editors to be very open to any suggestions I make too. And boring? Never! In the past few years I've written about the scariest theme park ride in the world; why cows' burps are increasing the levels of greenhouse gases in New Zealand; aquanauts living under the sea for extended periods; and high fashion for dogs – all have been total fun to research and write about.

When your beloved child comes home from school and presents you with the evening's homework reading, you can be assured that they are going to gain from that reading. Because to produce the 50 or so words in that little book, a lot of people – educational experts, designers, editors, illustrators, and writers – have put in a lot of time and effort to deliver a meaningful learning experience.

BOOKS FOR BEGINNING READERS

The 'story' books below are good to read alongside school readers as they contain high-frequency words and pictures that act as hints for the text.

That's Not My series by Fiona Watt, illustrated by Rachel Wells (Usborne)

I Went Walking by Sue Williams, illustrated by Julie Vivas (Turtleback Books, 1992)

Dog In, Cat Out by Gillian Rubinstein, illustrated by Ann James (Omnibus Books, 1991)

One Woolly Wombat by Kerry Argent (Scholastic Australia, 2012)

Spot series by Eric Hill (Penguin Books)

Crocodile Beat (First Readers edition) by Gail Jorgensen, illustrated by Patricia Mullins (Scholastic Australia, 2015)

Deadly Reads for Deadly Readers (four-book pack) by Nola Turner-Jensen, illustrated by Dub Leffler and Maggie Prewett (Magabala Books, 2012)

DIGITAL TECHNOLOGIES SUPPORTING BEGINNING READERS

There is a complex relationship between paper and digital books, and the way educators use digital technology to teach literacy concepts is continually being researched and debated.[4] There is no doubt that technology-infused experiences of literacy are reshaping learning environments and the contemporary reading practices of children. The rate at which digital change is occurring requires us to be flexible in our thinking but mindful of how quickly we move to the next 'bright shiny digital thing' offered to us and our children or students.

BOOKS FOR EMERGING READERS

Some books for little readers who are just starting their independent reading journey and can read a text with little or no assistance.

Did You Take the B From My _ook by Matt Stanton and Beck Stanton (and others in series) (Harper Collins, 2016)

Treehouse series by Andy Griffiths, illustrated by Terry Denton (Pan Macmillan Australia)

Billie B Brown series and Hey Jack series by Sally Rippin (Hardie Grant Egmont)

Aussie Nibbles series (various authors) (Puffin Books)

Solo series (various authors) (Scholastic Australia)

Ginger Green, Playdate Queen series by Kim Kane, illustrated by Jon Davis (Hardie Grant Egmont)

Toocool series by Phil Kettle, illustrated by Craig Smith (Scholastic Education)

Sporty Kids series by Felice Arena, illustrated by Tom Jellett (Penguin Books Australia)

Mates: Great Australian Yarns series (various authors) (Scholastic Australia)

Flying High (Scholastic Australia, 2015), *Going Bush with Grandpa* (Omnibus Books, 2014), *The Memory Shed* (Scholastic Australia, 2015) and *One Rule for Jack* (Omnibus Books, 2014) by Sally Morgan and Ezekiel Kwaymullina, illustrated by Craig Smith

The ease that young children have navigating hyperlinks, scrolling, enlarging and shrinking text and selecting elements is remarkable, and the engagement and delight they exhibit when making sense of digital texts through touch is reason enough to embrace technology as part of literacy learning. The use of touch-screen technology takes us back to the very early book experiences of babies, where touch is all-important in accessing and making meaning from a text. Technology affords the opportunity for the child to have some control over the reading experience as they play around with different but interconnected genres of text such as captions, images and embedded sound.

There are a number of digital literacy programs designed specifically for children. All need to be critically assessed before they are used, based on the needs and interests of the individual child. Many of these programs market themselves as superior to a paper-based literacy education approach. In reality, the research indicates that technology is at its best when woven through existing evidence-based, high quality literacy programs that employ a range of teaching and learning tools, both print and digital.[5] Digital reading programs or apps focusing on early word recognition or early reading of texts enable students to control their learning pace and to feel a sense of responsibility and autonomy in the process. In a busy classroom or home environment, independent computer work can provide individuals or small groups the time to complete work without direct adult instruction, and they are rewarded with immediate feedback. The immediacy of results can be highly motivating for students and frees the teacher to focus more directly on other areas of need in the classroom.

Literacy lessons in early years classrooms will have groups of students working in multiple ways: with a print text perhaps led by the teacher; using audio devices to listen to a fluid reading of a text to help them pronounce and understand words they are unable to read independently; on tablets completing word recognition or levelled reading programs and outside writing sentences on the wall with chalk. No single teaching strategy is better than another in terms of benefit but the use of multiple strategies ensures that learning styles, needs and paces are well catered for. Digital technologies are part of the modern day suite of teaching and learning strategies available to parents and educators.

Technology gives teachers the opportunity to have multiple reading strategies existing in the one learning space which means they are able to tailor learning to the needs of the individual.

ENCOURAGING WRITING AND ILLUSTRATION

As young children learn to read words, they also learn to make pencil marks on paper creating words and images. Reading, writing and illustrating are intrinsically linked. When a child begins to create meaningful text and recognisable images to communicate with others, it is a time of wonder and excitement, and a concrete example that they are comprehending and *creating* texts.

I distinctly remember author/illustrator and dear friend Narelle Oliver looking at PudStar's curly, whirly, twirly, upside-down and back-to-front handwriting and saying to me, 'Grab that handwriting, Megan! Keep it! You will never get that once she starts school and learns "proper handwriting". Graphic artists would kill to be able to properly re-create a child's natural handwriting.' Being someone who can't stand bits of 'mess' I did *not* follow Narelle's wise advice and keep samples of PudStar's 'fancy handwriting', as she used to call it. Narelle was right and these days PudStar is all about 'proper handwriting' with no swirls on the end – so boring, really. Narelle sadly passed away and is dearly missed by many, but I often think about her when I tuck away some of my younger daughter's 'fancy handwriting'.

It was the same with PudStar's artwork. As soon as she started formal education and learnt about the 'proper' way to draw, all the gorgeous twirly bird pictures she used to create with Narelle Oliver and the insightful sketches of family members stopped. I knew it was just a stage and that her confidence in her creativity and her ideas would return as she learnt new art techniques, but it also felt like the beginning of the end.

My mum, also a teacher librarian and former high school art teacher, has great conversations with all her grandchildren about their artworks. A while ago, PudStar was totally frustrated that she could not draw something exactly as she saw it. Mum was very patient in encouraging her to not think of her drawings as photographs – that drawings are not about making perfect images because we have cameras for that. She talked about art as being a different way of looking at something and capturing its essence. We have a beautiful picture book about Monet and my mother showed PudStar how Monet captured the movement and sparkle of water and flowers with dabs of paint. I often think about this conversation and retell it to my children and students when we are illustrating stories.

Having a supply of art and writing materials and unlined paper is key in encouraging spontaneous bursts of creative writing and drawing in little people. Both my girls have always had unlined journals next to their beds and a lead pencil or two (never a Sharpie pen – I learnt that the hard way). I never comment on what they write or draw unless asked. Blank paper is perfect for children of all ages as it encourages them to think outside those terribly restrictive red and blue lines. When there is no pressure to write or draw, children will often do their best and most creative work.

Encouraging children to draw, write, make, create and tinker is the perfect way to help them to develop their own unique style and embrace their 'art mistakes', which are not mistakes at all. Writing and illustration should be supported alongside reading as a means of encouraging a holistic approach to nuturing a literate child who is self-motivated to both consume and create words and images.

CHAPTER THREE

THE SCHOOL LIBRARY

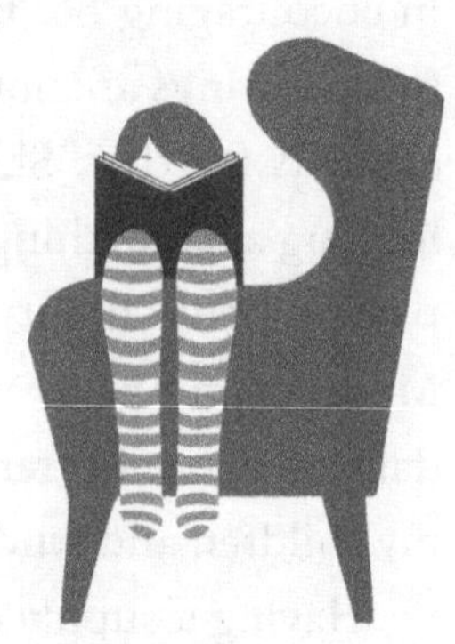

THE SCHOOL LIBRARY AND THE TEACHER LIBRARIAN

Many parents and educators are aware that school libraries are facing challenges of budget and staffing cuts. This trend has been on the rise for some time, but I'm not one to worry too much about trends. I think I rather like to buck them. I am also a firm believer that if you hold onto something for long enough it will come back in style, usually with a few tweaks that make it even better; in short, I reckon libraries are back in vogue. In the 1980s my mother bucked all fashion trends, and I remember being utterly mortified at her turning up to my rowing practice in zebra print jeans and Madonna sunglasses, long before these items were a thing. It is said that we turn into our mothers, and I have most certainly followed in her footsteps, both in becoming a teacher librarian and horrifying my children with my fashion choices.

I remain quietly confident that the 'trend' of looking at school libraries as an outdated resource is turning, especially where technology, Fab Labs and makerspaces are incorporated.[1] Well-resourced school libraries and quality teacher librarians are worth their weight in gold, and the positive impact they can have on an entire school community is well documented anecdotally and in research. Well-resourced school libraries, with exemplary teacher librarians and library support staff, develop and sustain a vibrant reading culture, promote innovative use of digital technologies and are a participatory hub within schools.

Stepping off my soapbox for a moment, what are the practicalities involved in ensuring the school in your community has a well-resourced library with passionate library staff who work to meet the curriculum and recreational needs of their patrons?

WHAT IS THE PURPOSE OF A SCHOOL LIBRARY?

School libraries exist as learning environments providing physical, digital and online spaces to enable access to high quality, diverse collections of resources, activities and services. These appropriately and ethically encourage and support the learning of all who engage with the space. Libraries are community resource centres and operate to contribute to the betterment of their customers, arming patrons with the information they require, and as a social space that can be used for cultural and educational events. School libraries vary in size, funding and staffing but all are focused on supporting student learning and creating lifelong learners and readers. School curriculums are resourced through the teacher librarian, who seeks to extend and support the individual curriculum, goals and ethos of their school environment. School libraries are wonderful places which are the beating heart of many school communities and a refuge for those who need time away from a busy school environment.

What should your school library look like?

A school library does not need an expensive fit-out or architecturally designed space. The very first school library I was put in charge of was a one-room demountable building in the middle of a dusty carpark at the back end of the primary school. Despite the distant location, it was such a hive of activity that we had to hand out numbered cards to monitor the number of students allowed inside at any one time. Those 'today you can visit the library at lunchtime' cards were as valuable as Golden Tickets to Willy Wonka's chocolate factory.

If you are a parent, carer or staff member, the following things are what I believe you should *expect* from your school library. It should:

- Be welcoming and inviting - the door and the entrance should invite the community inside.
- Be visible throughout the school. Being visible is not just about building placement, but also about excellent signage and presence both online (school website and social media) and in real life - for example, is your teacher librarian seen at all the major events at school?
- Have library staff who smile and are helpful because libraries are a service to the community. If your library staff are only ever behind a closed office door, you should consider removing that door or moving their work station to the front counter.
- Like a fast-food joint, your school library should be upselling at all times: 'Would you like a magazine with your loans this week?'
- Have a sense of order about them. I am all for chaos and my washing pile on the couch is a testament to this. Libraries, however, should be easy to navigate with resources that are ordered, searchable and findable. The Dewey decimal system exists for a reason and good library staff love a Dewey number on a book spine label.

- Have staff who continually weed and cull their collection with care. The classics will always remain under the careful eye of a good librarian or technician, but it is terribly difficult for young readers to find quality books when they are wedged between mouldy, dusty, horrid, ripped texts. Damaged or outdated books should be upcycled into artwork or lovingly recycled. Even if your library budget is dire, there is no need to hang on to 25 copies of a book that has not been borrowed since 1972.
- Have old and new technologies on display, such as QR codes for students to zap with their devices and stunning picture books treasured as works of art. Print and digital books can happily co-exist.
- Be comfortable, and have dedicated spaces for reading and for collaboration. Some students need downtime and solitude in a busy school day and libraries should provide this. They also need collaborative working spaces for sharing of ideas and creating together.
- Have some noise! I have had so many little kindy children over the years look up at me and say, 'You are TOO loud to be a library lady', but it doesn't take them long to realise that I am not the 'shhhhhhhhhh' style of librarian. Sure, libraries can be calm and quiet at times, but they can also be full of laughter, discussion and debate. If libraries have to be quiet, then I need a new job, as does my teaching partner because she is *way* louder than me.
- Be a fine example of a modern learning environment with 24/7 access to parts of the collection available to students through databases, ebooks and a functioning website, and possibly social media streams.

How do you know if you've struck a good teacher librarian?

Let's start at the beginning with what a teacher librarian actually is? I could just reproduce my job description, but real-life examples are far more engaging, so I'm going to use award-winning and well-known Australian teacher librarian Jenny Stubbs.

I first met Jenny when I was starting out as a teacher librarian. Jenny runs the vibrant Ipswich Teacher Librarian Network which, at her request, now has many local council librarians as members, adding greatly to the information pool. All teacher librarians across Australia are in networks because we are gatherers and sharers of information. One of the jobs of a librarian is to find and access information within a library, but the information gathering goes far beyond the walls of the physical building. Good librarians have curious and enquiring minds and collaborate with their colleagues and the community. Jenny is the master of surrounding herself with like-minded professionals and creatives who passionately believe in the power of story to change lives and the utter importance of literacy.

For over 28 years, the Ipswich Teacher Librarian Network has published a new book each year based on the Children's Book Council of Australia Book of the Year Awards, an enormous undertaking for a group of teacher librarians who work voluntarily on the project. This book is used in schools throughout Australia and overseas to promote Book Week and to provide resources to teachers and teacher librarians which support joyous and educationally sound exploration of some of the best books in the country.

Jenny Stubbs is the founder of the StoryArts Festival Ipswich, a biennial festival which has become one of the most highly regarded children's literature festivals in Australia. She advocates and builds effective library and literary programs that contribute to the development of young readers. Jenny and her team of dedicated volunteers organise and fund the festival largely through sales of the Ipswich Teacher Librarian Network book, and the festival has enabled tens of thousands of children to experience books and be inspired creatively through a series of free author events.

Jenny embraces any new technology that improves access to information and to story. For example, she introduced the first online chats in Australia between authors and children, which grew into an online literature festival that now caters for thousands of young people each year. She is a role model for lifelong learning.

As you can see, being a teacher librarian involves far more than returning books to shelves.

It must be acknowledged that not all school libraries are managed by teacher librarians, but by teachers, library technicians or other support staff. While a qualified teacher librarian remains the ultimate goal, we should never dismiss the work of others in the library. All dedicated staff can make a valuable contribution.

THE SCHOOL LIBRARY AS A SOCIAL HANGOUT

I can't tell you how many times I've had parents concerned that their child is at the library. Every. Single. Lunchtime. Alone, 'just' reading, usually down the back at the non-fiction shelves where it's nice and quiet. Sometimes I would like to join them. I don't know if other library staff do this, but I do gently 'shoo' some of these students from the library to go and run in the sun with their peers because a life lived in moderation is a good one. There are students I allow to come to the library only three days a week so that they have a healthy mix of exercise of the mind, body and social network. There are parents and carers who worry their child reads too much, and there are parents and carers who would give their right arm to have a child who reads.

A library is a beautiful place to work and play in and there are many reasons students seek them out.

- To escape the noise of the school playground, although as many of my students will tell you, I am the loudest librarian in the world, so don't come to my library for silence. I recently had a Year Six girl say to me, 'Mrs Daley, can we talk about books another time? I'm actually trying to read.' It's dreadful being shushed by your own students.
- Life is busy and schools are *really* busy. A lunchtime spent in the library can be much-needed downtime in a chaotic day.
- Like-minded peers and adults tend to reside in the library at lunchtime and friendships are often formed here.
- From the comfort of the school library, the mind can travel to China, the moon, the future, the past – very reassuring for little people who may be having problems in the actual world.

If you do have a child or student who is overly attached to the library, I'd recommend you talk to their teacher about some 'time out' from the library and how they can help make the playground more inviting for your child. It's also a good idea to make yourself known to your school library staff. Over the years, I've become really friendly with some of the parents of 'my library kids', mainly because the parents are also readers and lovers of libraries and so are part of my tribe.

If your school library has a makerspace zone or something similar, by golly, get your reader involved! The sharing of ideas, discussion, debate, problem-solving and working with others that occurs in these spaces are essential social and life skills to develop.

SELECTING QUALITY BOOKS

Australia has an incredibly diverse, vibrant and fabulous children's literary community that produces some of the best children's books in the world. But some people find that when they're presented with an entire wall of books in a store or a library it can be hard to choose and it all becomes a little overwhelming. I choose a children's book in a similar way to how I choose wine; my eye is drawn to the label and its design, then I am won over by how many shiny gold award stickers adorn it, then I consider the price point. For choosing children's books which will be loved, here are my tips.

Literary awards do matter. They point us in the right direction. Awards lists always spark conversation and controversy but these lists are a 'who's who' of children's and young adult books.

Phone a friend. Seriously, go find yourself a book expert at your local school library, public library or bookstore. We bookish types relish opportunities to talk with young readers and recommend books that will keep them reading. Many independent bookstores have children's and YA book specialists on their teams. Public and school library staff are there to help you and if you come across an unhelpful librarian, please feel free to stomp up and down and complain because I strongly believe that we are in customer service and that readers are our customers. Much to the horror of my tween (actually everything I do horrifies her), if I spot a parent looking confused in a bookstore I usually sidle over to them and help out.

Judge a book by its cover. I do it. All. The. Time. If a book is well designed and the cover grabs you, it generally means that care and thought has gone into not just the cover but also the content. A great cover sums up an entire book in one image.

Price point. This could be controversial but on the whole I would prefer to purchase one exceptional hardcover children's book than four or five 'bargain bin' books. Bargain books tend to not remain treasured books and they are often mass-produced items that need a good edit, a better illustrator or a much better author. There are, of course, exceptions to this, like the time I found hardcover versions of Blue Willow china-inspired *Little Blue* (Gaye Chapman) reduced to a mere two dollars. After I wept inside that such a stunning book could possibly be reduced to so little, I purchased all 31 copies to use as party favours – way better than a lolly bag (said no child ever). If you cannot afford books or would prefer to try before you buy, then give your library card a workout.

Hover around groups of children. Not in a way that will cause concern, but stand near children in bookshops and libraries and watch what they are borrowing and listen to what books they are talking about. After all, young people are the very best guides to the books that will be enjoyed.

SELF-SELECTION

One of my work goals is that my primary school students will become efficient in self-selection of recreational material by high school. Teacher librarians seek to arm children with strategies for searching out books for themselves and quality library programming ensures that self-selection strategies are explicitly and incidentally taught from a young age.

In the early years, teaching self-selection strategies may take the form of browsing with children through forward-facing picture book boxes and talking about what appeals to them based on the cover. I model this, often through role-playing when choosing a book for myself: 'Oh, here is a book with a cat on the cover, I'll get that one! Oh, hang on ... I really don't like cats at all, I'm a dog person. This one has a lemon tree on the front and the colours remind me of being outside in my garden – this one I *will* borrow because I love gardening.' I have one-on-one conversations with students whenever I can and regularly insist that each kindy or prep child walks past their teacher or myself on the way out and tells us why they have chosen a particular book. We make a game of this 'march past' and the children hold up their book and loudly tell us why they think it looks like a 'good fit' for them.

There are also patterns when selecting books with young children. If a child has really enjoyed *The Very Cranky Bear* (Nick Bland), this is an opportunity to point out other Nick Bland books and see if children can see the similarities in illustrative style. Likewise, if a child continually borrows books on a particular subject, perhaps dinosaurs, introduce them to non-fiction texts, or expand their horizons and offer them some books on jungle animals – some children feel safe sticking with 'what they know' in books and have difficulty knowing what to move on to.

Throughout the primary school years, teachers, parents and students should have ongoing conversations about why and how we choose books for independent recreational reading. Empowering students to choose their own books sets them up for being lifelong readers and shifts ownership of reading from the adult to the child.

Questions that help with self-selection

- Does the subject matter appeal to you?
- Why do you want to read this book?
- Read the first page – do you understand most of the words?
- Is this book going to challenge you and are you interested enough to accept that challenge?
- Have you read anything else by this author and did you enjoy it?
- Tell me the last book you really enjoyed? Can you find something similar?

Strategies that help with self-selection

- Write down the authors you like and search out their titles.
- Check new book displays in libraries and bookstores.
- Scour the shelves at home and find things other family members have enjoyed.
- Talk with your peers about the books they like to read.
- Ask your friendly school or local librarian for some recommendations.
- Take your time browsing the library shelves and you might notice a gem that you have not seen before.

THE LIBRARY MAKERSPACE

This chapter would not and could not exist without Jackie Child AKA #bestteachingpartnerever. Jackie landed in my world and my library about eight years ago – my little teacher librarian life has never been the same, nor would I want it to be. I hired Jackie because I thought we were peas in a pod. Turns out we are polar opposites in just about everything except our passion for primary school education, and for children's literature, and our ability to talk our boss into letting us run with half-crazed ideas.

The half-crazed idea Jackie raised was to introduce some spanners, drills, and sewing equipment into the library. She'd seen this 'cool thing' at a conference where libraries in America were inviting the community to work collaboratively on projects that often involved engineering principles and skills; she believed it was a natural fit with school libraries where information is sourced, digitally and physically, and shared among peers. Jackie Child was a rally car driver, engine re-builder and a keen creator of ice-skating outfits *before* she was a teacher librarian, so I did wonder if she was trying to bring her own love of a good tool set into *my* pristine library.

Turned out Jackie was onto something and her name has become synonymous with the makerspace movement in Australia.

What is the makerspace movement?

This might sound like a buzzword but the concepts underpinning the makerspace movement are timeless and have been part of the makeup of libraries since their inception.[3] The idea of making, tinkering, engineering and creating is not a new one. Using these elements within a community space forms the conceptual framework for the term 'makerspace'. A makerspace mindset values questioning and inquiry, re-inventing and exploring new ways of doing, and focuses on participating in learning - making and re-purposing, rather than consuming.

Under the umbrella term of 'makerspace', there exists several incarnations of the idea, with the Massachusetts Institute of Technology (MIT) considered to be the first to formalise the concept in America. It is generally believed that the makerspace concept evolved from the hackerspaces in Germany as early as the 1950s.[4] One of the incarnations is Fab Labs, which are places of fabrication where physical items are produced. A hackerspace is focused on computers and technology and co-working spaces are shared working environments with shared tools and resources.[5]

Makerspaces are the perfect partnership for libraries - where information is stored, accessed, shared, explored, pondered and debated. Library patrons can follow their interests and passions, applying knowledge from all areas of their life; personal and educational knowledge, experiences and skills. Informal makerspace activities are probably already occurring in your school or local library; formalising the process is merely a response to what students and customers now expect from modern library spaces and extending our outreach to new library patrons.

Libraries provide equal access to information, resources and technologies and this is particularly obvious in public libraries, where patrons access the internet and computers, assisted in this process by library staff. Increasingly, libraries are housing and providing equal access to hardware such as robots, 3D printers and scanners. It follows that librarians embrace the ideas underpinning the makerspace movement and facilitate community interest in new and emerging technologies and spaces of making and creating.

In our school library, books have been the starting point for nearly all of our makerspace projects. Books with characters that think outside the square (such as the Violet Mackerel series by Anna Branford and Sarah Davis, *Different Like Coco* by Elizabeth Matthews, the Engibear series by Andrew King and Benjamin Johnston, and *Rosie Revere, Engineer* by Andrea Beaty and David Roberts) or books that present opportunities to create new characters or ideas, with technology or physical equipment. For example, when reading *A Very Unusual Pursuit* by Catherine Jinks, we invented our own Bogles, and when reading *Something Wonderful* by Raewyn Caisley and Karen Blair we created our own wonderful machines to solve a problem at home. Student borrowing of books and their engagement in reading has also increased since the introduction of a makerspace zone in the library. As students tinker and create, we observe incidental language learning and the building of literacy across multiple domains. The library has become a space for all, not just for students who identify as readers. When students enter our library space, they are surrounded by books to tempt all persuasions and more often than not they walk out with one or two books under their arm. Recently, students playing the *America the Wild* game on our Xbox Kinect ended up walking out with the book *Call of the Wild* (Jack London); librarians are experts at finding the right book at the right time!

For many students who have struggled with literacy and for whom the library is not a space of contentment, the makerspace has been an opportunity to invite them in through a different 'doorway' and for them to shine. There are many different ways to come to a love of reading.

For more information on setting up of a makerspace, see the guide at the end of this book on 'How to create a library makerspace' (page 213).

BOOKS THAT SUPPORT THE MINDSET OF THE MAKERSPACE MOVEMENT

Different Like Coco by Elizabeth Matthews (Candlewick Press, 2007)

Rosie Revere, Engineer by Andrea Beaty, illustrated by David Roberts (Abrams Books for Young Readers, 2013)

Brobot by James Foley (Fremantle Press, 2016)

Engibear's Dream by Andrew King, illustrated by Benjamin Johnston (Little Steps, 2012)

Engibear's Bridge by Andrew King, illustrated by Benjamin Johnston (Little Steps, 2014)

Something Wonderful by Raewyn Caisley, illustrated by Karen Blair (Penguin, 2016)

Beautiful Oops by Barney Saltzberg (Workman, 2010)

Marvelous Mattie: How Margaret E. Knight Became an Inventor by Emily Arnold McCully (Farrar, Straus and Girou, 2006)

Violet the Pilot by Steve Breen (Dial Books for Young Readers, 2008)

Ish by Peter H. Reynolds (Walker Books, 2005)

Have Fun, Molly Lou Melon by Patty Lovell, illustrated by David Catrow (Putnam, 2012)

Young Frank: Architect by Frank Viva (Museum of Modern Art, 2013)

Mechanica: A beginner's field guide by Lance Balchin (Five Mile Press, 2016)

Zeroes & Ones by Cristy Burne (Brio Books, 2018)

LITERARY AWARDS

There are many literary awards in Australia shining the light on the best books for children and young adults. The Children's Book Council of Australia (CBCA) Book of the Year Awards is possibly the most long-standing and well-regarded for recognising the talent of authors and illustrators in this country. The awards were established in 1946 with the first winners receiving a camellia flower before generous donations guaranteed a financial prize for each category. The CBCA award stickers carry weight in terms of literary honour. The Shortlist and Notables List of the CBCA Awards are used by many parents, teachers and children as a buying guide.

Many other awards fill the literary calendar. Some awards are state-based, while others are more niche and can be hugely beneficial when looking for books of a certain genre or topic. Two examples of niche children's book awards are the Environment Award for Children's Literature, which awards books promoting themes of sustainability and nature, and the Aurealis Awards, which recognise the achievements of Australian science fiction, fantasy and horror.

Each category of an award usually contains a large range of books, suitable for different age groups within that category, and parents/teachers should always assess the themes and content of an individual book before choosing it for their child or classroom. Do not assume that the 'picture book category' will contain books suitable for infants, with many illustrated texts being more suitable for older readers. It is also important to keep in mind that literary awards are based on the literary merit of each book and are not children's choice/popular awards.

Young readers are able to take part in recognising the books they love best with a number of children's choice awards co-existing within Australia. These awards are an opportunity for readers to make their voices heard. When we ask young people to evaluate their favourite books for an award, we involve them in their reading in a way that asks them to think critically about reading and writing in general, and we provide them with a sense of ownership in choosing the winners themselves.

CHILDREN'S BOOK COUNCIL OF AUSTRALIA BOOK WEEK

CBCA Book Week is the longest-running children's festival in Australia and is managed by the Children's Book Council of Australia (CBCA). The announcement of the winners of the CBCA Book of the Year Awards kicks off CBCA Book Week and it is a week of celebrating Australian children's and young adult literature. To be honest, most of us stretch the celebrations out for an entire term with author visits, book fairs, competitions, maker fairs and events in our school communities as well as attending many children's literature functions.

The theme for Book Week is set by the CBCA and each year an award-winning illustrator is engaged to bring the theme to life. Illustrators interpret the theme in their own style, ensuring that each year the posters, banners, balloons and stickers are as individual and unique as each picture book on a shelf. This sends librarians and educators off on happy shopping trips to turn their libraries or classrooms into reading islands, galaxies or deserts, depending on the theme. Libraries and bookstores in your local area will almost certainly be celebrating CBCA Book Week. Following the social media accounts of your local library and independent bookstore will guarantee that you don't miss a single literary event.

My mother had the pleasure of being the national merchandise manager for the CBCA for several years and it was an honour to peek behind the scenes. One year she worked with the late Gregory Rogers on the merchandise and his take on the theme 'One World, Many Stories' aligned closely to his book that had won the picture book category in the previous year. His series of illustrations for that theme remains among my favourites. CBCA Book Week posters have become collector's items and everyone has opinions on which posters were the greatest. I use past posters over and over again in my library and also as artwork in my children's bedrooms.

Book Week competitions and dress-up parades are always a key part of term three in Australian schools – and the costumes can be as simple or as elaborate as time and craftiness will allow. Discuss which book characters your child would like to dress up as and take it from there. It's fantastic if your child can have ownership over the costume choice and be involved in the creation – just make sure they take inspiration from a book, not their favourite movie or digital game! My 'How to create a Book Week costume' guide (page 217) is a good starting point if you need a creative nudge.

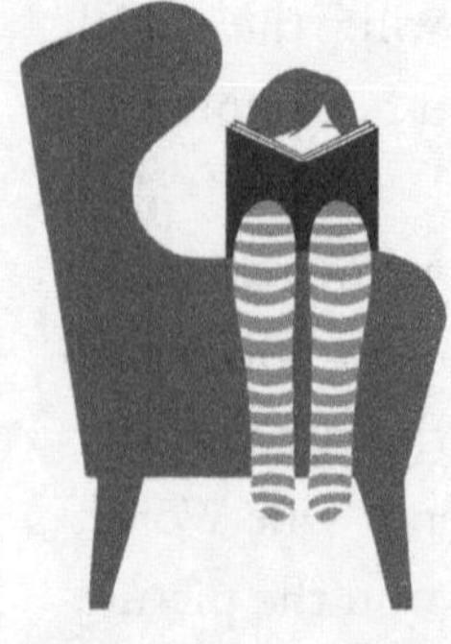

CHAPTER FOUR

SPACES FOR READING

Whether in the home, classroom, kindergarten or library, creating a space all about reading emphasises books and their beauty to children. This can be as important as the learning and language tools an educator uses. Take a look at your child's kindy or school classroom next time you are there. See all the labels? The signage? The posters with words and pictures? That is what we call a 'print-rich environment'. A print-rich home helps young children become familiar with letters, numbers, pictures and words. It tells young children that print is important and has a purpose. My mantra for creating a print-rich environment is: *Display print. Use print. Value print.*

I love nothing better than walking into a kindergarten or childcare centre and being drawn into a fabulous reading space. Libraries with dedicated spaces designed for children are my happy places – and I've been known to say that I could move into my local library book nook. In the homes of my friends I'll be found checking out the books on the shelves in their kids' rooms and gushing over big, comfy reading chairs. I may not notice the designer entry table, but I will always notice the reading spaces and bookshelves.

I don't think there is any better home décor than beautiful books and prints from favourite picture books. I am slowly amassing a collection of original artwork from books and I regularly tell the students at school that 'when I grow up' I'm going to own an art gallery dedicated to picture book endpapers. I'm also a big fan of forward-facing storage for children's books because not only are the covers works of art and deserve to be on display, but the books are easily identifiable, helping young readers to self-select.

How you organise your books within your space is entirely up to you. I'd love nothing better than my home being organised like my school library but that won't happen. Nor will I ever organise my books by colour because my librarian brain cannot cope with the idea that *A Clockwork Orange* (Anthony Burgess) could sit on a shelf next to *Winnie-the-Pooh* (A. A. Milne). Having said this, my Dewey decimal system-loving library technician has colour coded her books in her new home. We cannot discuss it at work as I am too shocked that a devotee of library rules would do such a thing!

BOOK-THEMED BEDROOMS

Surrounding your child in print and visual-rich spaces is a great way to model your love of books and reading. My children have had book-themed bedrooms several times in their short little lives. Book-themed rooms are a no-brainer to me as the colour themes, motifs and décor items you choose are decided by the artwork of the illustrator of your favourite picture book or from the world created by your favourite author.

My second child started life with a nursery based on one of my all-time favourite picture books, *Little Blue* (Gaye Chapman), which also inspired her middle name. Heavily pregnant at a Children's Book Council of Australia conference, I saw the Little Hare publisher stand filled with heavenly posters and postcards from the book and fell hard for it. The book retells the story of the Willow pattern plates. In creating a *Little Blue*-themed room, I used blue-and-white Chinese paintings, as well as a gorgeous soft gum-tree green. This is still my favourite bedroom theme as it was soft and calming – until the very loud, screaming-with-reflux-pain baby was added (I am still recovering from those first two years!). I also had a calico reading tent with Willow pattern cushions and a thick lambswool rug, bunting made from the pages of the book (yes, I cut up a copy) and cot linen in Willow pattern fabric. I colour-matched the blue of the book at a hardware store so the walls were painted the palest and prettiest of blues.

But don't feel as though you have to go to such great lengths. A reading space can be as simple as a chair or window seat near a bookshelf or even a great big bean bag with a basket of books beside it. No matter your budget, a reading nook can always be created.

Kelly McDonough from *The Styling Mama* is an expert in spaces for children, tweens and families. Kelly has shared some thoughts on home design and how to maximise a space for a reading. These ideas can be easily adapted for the classroom or school library.

Kelly McDonough

If I think back to my childhood I remember standing in front of our huge timber bookshelf. It wasn't fancy. I actually didn't even notice the shelves because, let's be honest, kids don't care if it's a designer piece or if you picked it up at a garage sale. They only see the things they love on the shelves.

With such an abundance of home décor inspiration in stores, renovation TV shows and online, it can be way too easy to become lost in the big-ticket items such as the on-trend 'must have' pieces. These might fill the void (or the room) but there is one thing to remember: they aren't long-term items and they probably won't be part of your child's memories. Books, on the other hand, are stayers. Stories defy age and continue to create an environment that inspires imagination, touches our soul and educates little minds.

Shelving

If you're short on floor space, think up. Shelving is not only versatile, but it's gorgeous and timeless. I love using picture ledges down low so that little hands can find favourite books. Think about retail store displays: the stuff they want seen is kept at eye level. Books shelved spine-out just end up being pulled off bookshelves and left on the floor; books shelved face-out are easily identifiable by their covers so they not only invite the reader to pick them up but also create an instant display.

If you're lacking in toy storage space, some funky baskets or boxes on the shelves is a great way to keep books tidy and stored when they're not being used. And a little tip – rotate the boxes around so that there is always something different on the eye-level shelf your kids go to first.

Colour

Using colour in spaces for kids is like breathing: it happens without thinking. Kids are naturally drawn to colour, but that doesn't necessarily mean a colour assault on the eyes. My advice with choosing colours is to pick three main ones. These could be anything from your child's favourite colour, to a favourite book cover with a dominant colour or a chair or quilt cover in the space.

Once you have these three colours choose three more variations to tie everything together. For example, adding a soft grey to a bright blue will help balance it out. Experiment with sample paint wheels to see what works and challenge yourself to think outside your usual go-to combinations. You'll be surprised at the colours that work together! At the end of your search you'll have six colours to work with. Having different shades of your chosen colours actually helps avoid the room becoming too matchy-matchy, making it kid-friendly and versatile when it comes time to mix things up.

Zones

A reading nook doesn't have to be sized to epic proportions. A cosy cushion and a basket with books placed on a rug or under a canopy draws little eyes instantly. Kids are funny little creatures as they will seek out spaces we don't think of. So don't be afraid to get your child onboard with mapping out a zone. While it's probably not a great move to get them to design the whole layout, seeing a room or area from their perspective might help you to plan and visualise what works best for your child. Well, for that day anyway!

And if you're lacking floor space, areas can always have a double purpose. A little trolley on wheels containing arts and crafts can be brought out to create an instant makerspace and then easily packed away again!

Kids' spaces are about functionality. Your budget, tastes and the purpose of the room are all factors to consider when decorating. Planning out your storage options, zones and colours aren't the be-all, but they are a great place to start when designing an area that you and the kids will all love.

I wish I had a solution for a room that automatically cleans itself – I promise you'll be the first to know if I work that one out!

As Kelly mentions above, kids may seek out spaces that seem like odd choices to us as adults. I witness it daily in my school library as children read under desks or in the middle of rows of shelving. Each year I ask my Year Three to Year Six students to close their eyes and imagine their perfect reading space, thinking about its colours, furniture, comfort, sounds and 'feel'. Students write a description and then we either paint or draw this space. If we have time, we create a model using materials from our makerspace. I always imagined that beds would be the favoured reading place of choice, but I am constantly amazed by the variety of spaces children describe. They commonly desire a small and cosy space, often on the floor or under something (tent, blanket, bed, etc) and for it to feel tranquil and calm. Every year a number of children will describe an outside space, such as in a tree or on a deck, and a few children will express a preference for reading on a bus or other crowded space like a shopping centre – usually explaining that they read to 'block out' the overwhelming sensory experience of such environments. The message here is that what we adults see as ideal or appropriate reading spaces may in fact not work for every reader. Having a discussion with your child or going though a creative exercise as described above can uncover some valuable insights into the readers in your care.

THE READING CLASSROOM

Classrooms need an area or zone dedicated to recreational reading. I vividly recall my first year of teaching and the reading zone I created in my Year Two classroom because I think it remains my favourite to this day: acres of deep purple and bright turquoise tulle, ten oversized turquoise cushions covered in purple stars (thank you, Nan, for making those), framed pages torn out of old books and a selection of beautiful books that I changed each week at the school library and displayed in baskets and on the windowsill. When I eventually moved from the classroom to the library, the tulle came with me and my first library was a riot of colour and texture (but, I promise, not an assault to the eyes because I did stick to just a few colours – clearly I have missed my calling as a home stylist).

While there are some fabulous reading spaces in classrooms all over Instagram and Pinterest, I think it's important that you work with the interests of the students and allow them to create the space with you. It can even become a curriculum-related task. The main things for students to think about should be how the books will be arranged, how key books will be displayed and 'advertised', how to make the space comfortable (chairs, cushions or bean bags), how often books will be changed and by whom, and what colours or innovative features should be used to invite and welcome readers to the space. When the students are a part of the process, it gives them a sense of ownership and they are more likely to feel comfortable using the space. This is also a perfect way to involve reluctant readers in a reading-related task that will have a positive outcome for everyone.

How you stock your classroom library is also an important consideration and books should be changed up regularly to keep interest high. With most of the classroom libraries at school, we library staff send new books each term ensuring a mix of fiction, non-fiction, chapter books and illustrated texts. There are also a number of classrooms where students are assigned the weekly task of 'librarians'. These students manage the books in the classroom reading zone and swap some out each week, tidy them and refresh displays.

INVITING LIBRARY SPACES

School library spaces are public spaces and should consider the needs of the learners as well as the needs of the educators and the entire school community. Our students need a balance of spaces from expansive, active and social to small, intimate and quiet with technology infused rather than glaringly obvious.[1] Teachers need spaces to withdraw individual students for testing and areas for whole class research. Social learning spaces might be needed for small groups to discuss and debate or for students to read aloud in a group context. Conversely, students also appreciate and seek refuge from a busy day in small reading nooks and quiet, reflective spaces.

In *33 Educational Design Principles for Schools and Community Learning Centres*, Lackney talks of creating 'alcoves for learning' centrally located and close to resources.[2] I love this term and it brings to mind cosy and inviting learning spaces. Many of you will fondly remember those individual, 'walled' library desks from your own school days; your own little private space where you were meant to work in silence. These went out of vogue as education embraced group work, but more recently we have reconsidered the needs of individuals, and for many students there are moments in a school day when being alone (as alone as one can be in a busy school) can be beneficial to think, create and wonder.[3] In my own school library, we created 'booths' reminiscent of milk bar booths where students can work alone or in small groups. They are close to the fiction area of the library and often students choose a book and make themselves comfortable in a booth for study or for recreational reading. These 'alcoves for learning' have probably been the best feature of our library despite the initial worry that they would look a little like school libraries of old!

I could talk endlessly about the importance of displays of books in the library, but instead I'm going to distil this information down to one sentence that I hope will stick in your mind: Library displays should be dotted around the library, be ever-changing, professional (quit the clipart), eye-catching with all books facing forwards and able to be borrowed from the display. (If you're so inclined you can find plenty of ideas and inspiration on Pinterest for themed library displays.)

A final point on library spaces: if at all possible, extend your space into the outdoors (see chapter 11 for more on this). Our school library is the top level of a building, which is not ideal, but we utilise the lovely outdoor areas downstairs for quiet reading, group reading and workshopping. Currently we are doing a unit of work on mindful reading, and many of the students choose to read near our native stingless beehives or in the grove of palm trees.

I am very fortunate to work in a dynamic and constantly evolving library space, which we consider to be meeting the many requirements of a modern learning environment by promoting and supporting a range of pedagogies, including delivering, applying, communicating and creating. Our library offers flexibility and access to the varied resources to support a technologically robust community and one which promotes language and literacy learning at all times.

CHAPTER FIVE

THE RIGOUR OF READING

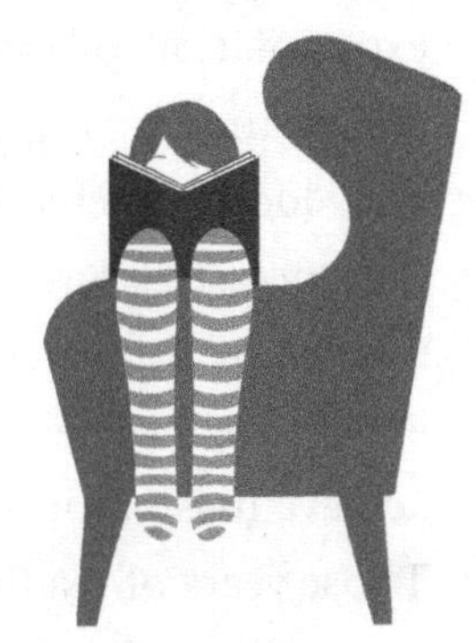

A level of literacy is important in successfully navigating life and becoming an informed, active and contributing member of society. Many of us know from anecdotal evidence that sustained and regular reading, as well as reading for pleasure, contributes to positive academic outcomes, and this is backed by research examining how reading correlates to academic success.[1] We want young people to be highly literate and critical consumers of words; from the novels they read to environmental signage on the streets to marketing images and the analysis required for understanding complex ethical issues. Deep and meaningful reading contributes to language acquisition and the ability to use language in a way that is empowering. But how do we maintain rigour in reading while ensuring that we don't turn reading into a chore? What motivates students to read and continue reading?

As children move into the upper primary years of schooling their reading, by necessity, becomes more purposeful and strategic. The demands of the school curriculum require students to read a large volume of materials, and this only increases as students move into high school. Those who have read with enthusiasm from a young age and have built up a powerful armoury of reading comprehension strategies are in an ideal position to cope with the demands of reading for academic gain. These students build on prior knowledge, and are prepared for rich and thought-provoking analysis and skilled extrapolation of information using techniques such as skimming and scanning, highlighting passages, taking notes, summarising and locating credible supporting sources. Readers understand sentence structure and know where in a paragraph the important nugget of information will be, and they read widely in order to extend their general knowledge, build an extensive vocabulary and achieve mastery in what they read and in the tasks they complete.[2] Those years of reading for pleasure and racing through novels at an astonishing pace pay dividends when high school arrives and the reading volume increases.

Reading for pleasure need not disappear in high school. Fantasy is a great way for teens to escape mathematics study, for example. Or some young people may be comforted by reading contemporary realism stories of students who, like them, feel overwhelmed by a heavy workload but manage to stumble their way through school and social situations. A ready supply of age-appropriate novels in the house will ensure that in moments of downtime your child will have a book to provide them with a portal to another world outside of study and school. Reading newspapers, magazines and graphic novels can also be used as escapism literature. The ability to dip in and out of these short-grab texts can suit busy students, satisfying their need for a quick and interesting read.

A word of caution here to not push your avid reader too much. I can put my hand up for being guilty of this and it really serves no purpose; in fact, it can turn reading from a pleasure to a chore. At all times and in all situations, make reading a joy and remember that even the most avid of readers may go through a rut.

EXTENDING YOUR CHILD'S READING

Once your child hits a certain reading level in those early years of primary school, they will start to crave books with more complex storylines and in their area of passion, be it sharks, fairies, magical tales or true stories of heroes. This is a time when things can come unstuck for parents and educators alike and we stress over questions like: 'What on earth can I give them next?'; 'How do I know what's appropriate?'; 'I know they are only five, but can they read Harry Potter?'; 'Shouldn't they read the classics I read as a child!'

I am of the opinion that reading material should always be age appropriate; however, there are various schools of thought on this, with many parents happy to allow their children full access to their home or public library collection. You know your child best so you are the one best placed to make the decision on their level of reading maturity. In my role as a teacher librarian, I often spend time talking to parents who are keen to extend their child's reading with books aimed at a much older audience. I always point out that while their five- or six-year-old might technically be able read every word in, say, Harry Potter with great fluency, they may not grasp the content and full complexity of the story, and it always seems such a shame to me to not completely fall in love with a series like Harry Potter. The same can be said for something like *The Wind in the Willows* (Kenneth Grahame) or *Black Beauty* (Anna Sewell). If read at too young an age, while the child may understand the words, they may not fully appreciate the beauty of the language and, at worst, they may end up intensely disliking a fantastic book. The classics are wonderful for older readers but are a slog for young readers still working on the mechanics of reading. In my experience, books are usually only great when they are read by the intended age group, though there are always exceptions to this.

With young people who have an insatiable reading appetite, I always ask parents to continue to encourage their capable reader with their classroom readers as these are designed to teach specific skills, and while they may appear 'too easy' for your child, they serve a purpose. I also urge parents to never let their children leave picture books behind once they've 'moved on' to chapter books. If I had a dollar for every child who said to me, 'Mummy says I have to borrow chapter books because I can read now and don't need picture books', I would be well and truly retired and living in Bali. Picture books have come a long way since our own childhood memories of them. The language in today's picture books is often complex and at a much higher level than that found in an early chapter book, and the storylines sophisticated and thought-provoking. And we haven't even considered the illustrations yet! We live in an age of visuals; picture books teach visual literacy like no other teaching tool (see chapter 10). Avid young readers are often the ones most capable of dealing with the complexity of a picture book ... I could go on and on. Suffice to say, I believe that every child should always have picture books on the go.

There are so many young readers whose reading ability and comprehension is way beyond their years and they can wield a pen as effortlessly as many published authors. While this sounds glorious to many parents, it can be quite the struggle to keep the gifted child engaged and connected with their learning. Tracey Hand, co-founding director of Optimise Learning, has years of experience as a teacher and a particular passion for the learning needs of gifted and talented students. I admire her work very much and have been fortunate to call her a colleague. She has the following advice for parents looking to extend their gifted children.

Tracey Hand

It is commonly accepted that the experience of childhood has significantly changed for the twenty-first century child. Many people of my generation recall the sense of fun and freedom that came with being allowed to play outside with the neighbours' kids all day, usually unsupervised, until 'Mum called you to come in for tea'. Books could be described as the 'last frontier' for today's child. Stepping into a book may be the only opportunity many children have now to experience the thrill of adventure and the sense that 'anything could happen'. In my mind, books play a vital role in enriching the life of a child – today more than ever.

As a specialist 'gifted and talented' teacher, I am often asked by parents to recommend 'suitable' books for their gifted reader. My advice to parents is to assist their child to seek out books that cater for their interests and ability level while keeping in mind that many age-appropriate books often lack the depth and complexity young gifted children crave. By monitoring their child's book choices and providing them with the opportunity to indulge their passion for reading, parents are enabling their child's imagination, creativity and critical thinking skills to flourish.

To help extend avid readers you can:

1. Support your child's passion for reading by exposing them to a wide variety of text types and topics that will engage them, challenge them, teach them and arouse their curiosities while encouraging them to think deeply and ponder. Providing your avid reader with a wide variety of books is similar to providing them with a drink to quench their thirst.
2. Ensure that your avid reader is engaging with books that contain age-appropriate themes and concepts. Many avid readers have the ability to read books written for students much older than they are, which can cause them to become distressed or feel confused by what they have read. I recall a past student who at five years old had the reading age of a fifteen-year-old, and after finding and reading a short article titled 'Fearsome Facts: the Inca' in her school library, she was too traumatised to sleep in her own room for a few months. 'Why did the Incas kill children, Mummy?' was the question this young girl wanted answered.

3. Make the time to discuss with your child the books they are reading. Checking in will help you to keep abreast of the themes your child is being exposed to.
4. Unless your child objects, continue to read aloud to them regularly. There is an assumption that young gifted children do not need this, but reading aloud not only models reading but expands their book experience, especially if they are beginning to develop a preference for a specific genre at a young age.
5. Ensure you provide opportunities for your child to visit the local library regularly. Get to know your local librarian; they often love to help gifted readers indulge their particular interest and will recommend recently purchased books.

Reading aloud to capable readers is not something we often think to do but, as Tracey says, it should be continued as long as possible. It helps to build connection and community as readers discuss a shared experience of a book. It is also a great way to level the playing field, with readers of varied ability making meaning together and developing a shared culture of reading.

FROM READER TO WRITER

Research suggests a strong link between reading and writing competency and we know that readers are often the most capable writers. Reading and writing rely on many of the same cognitive processes and the skills reinforce and support each other.[3] One of the ways I often extend my capable readers is through writing, often in response to books they have been reading either recreationally or for school. Crafting a narrative or penning some poetry fully immerses children in the writing and reading cycle. At school I have, for many years now, worked with small groups of students on extending their writing skills, based on their reading interest or on a book we have chosen together to study. We have innovated on particular texts, co-authored books online with other extension students from local schools, and have contacted favourite authors to interview them about their creative writing process. Creative writing skills and academic writing skills are interconnected and interchangeable, and an extensive vocabulary built through wide reading empowers young people in all forms of writing.

Allison Tait, author of The Mapmaker Chronicles and Ateban Cipher series, is a talented children's author. Her work at the Australian Writers' Centre (AWC) in helping others to realise their dream of becoming an author is outstanding, as is the AWC podcast she co-hosts with Valerie Khoo, *So You Want to be a Writer*. When my husband Dan passed away, Allison organised authors and other literary folk to take over my blog for more than six months, until I was ready to take it back up – I will never forget this incredible act of kindness. Allison was the first person who came to mind when I wanted someone to comment on the connection between reading and writing.

Allison Tait

'If you can't see it, you can't be it.' This phrase is generally used in regard to role-modelling careers, but I think it works just as well when it comes to reading and writing. When authors are asked for their top tips for writers, their number one response – and I can vouch for this because I host a podcast in which I've asked hundreds of authors for their top tips – is 'READ'. If someone asks who inspired me to become an author, I talk about the hundreds of books I read as a child.

If someone asks me how I understand story structure, pacing, dialogue and narrative arcs, I explain that most of what I do is innate, instinctive. Why?

Because of the thousands of books I've read in my lifetime, both as an adult and as a child. I've read detective stories and romance stories and adventure stories and stories that were beautifully written but didn't even seem to HAVE a story.

Through reading those thousands of books I have absorbed things that I love – and things that I didn't. I have studied, without ever knowing I was doing it, the craft of writing at the hands of masters such as J. R. R. Tolkien, Margaret Atwood, Stephen King, Jane Austen, Judy Blume, S. E. Hinton, Charles Dickens, Mark Twain and [insert the name of your favourite author here because chances are I've read his or her work].

From non-fiction books I have learnt that one tiny fact can be the most interesting thing in a sea of words. From comics I have learnt the importance of a single idea per panel to keep a story moving. From memoir I have learnt that any story can be riveting when the voice is honest and true. All of these things came together when I started writing The Mapmaker Chronicles series.

Kids who read know that a story needs a beginning, a middle and an end. They know that a story is not just a description – that something has to happen. Their vocabulary grows all the time, giving them new tools to use in their own writing.

Kids who read know what it is like to be dragged into another world and emerge blinking at the end of a book. When I explain in my school talks that one of the things I love most about writing is that it gives me the ability to control the whole world, they get it.

Reading fuels imagination, ideas, and imagery. Being read to has the same effect.

There is more to writing than simply reading. Every craft has its own set of tools, and writing is no different. But if you're a reader, you're not starting from scratch. You are simply building on the big picture that every single story you've read combines to create.

And who doesn't love a head start?

••

CHAPTER SIX

READING CHALLENGES

READING DIFFERENCES AND DIFFICULTIES

For many parents and educators supporting young people who learn to read differently and/or face challenges along the way, reading can become a daily battle, as can navigating the education system and advocating for a child. Whether a young person has diagnosed literacy issues or is a hardcore reluctant reader, it is just plain *hard* to be the adult watching from the sidelines and feeling quite helpless. Literacy issues are complex and multifaceted and, as many families will know, often where there is one diagnosed condition there can be another, further adding to the complexity.

I am not a specialist in teaching students who learn to read differently, but in my twenty years as an early years educator and teacher librarian I have worked alongside many individuals as they walked this journey. It is really important to note here that *everyone* has an individual reading and learning journey. I have been privileged to witness heart-warming stories of success but in other cases I have been left feeling like I have failed a child and that there is more I could have done, more we *all* could have done.

There is much misinformation surrounding the therapies and techniques that are best used when working with young people who learn to read differently. Many programs being talked about in the media have little or no evidence of success or research behind them but can convince devoted parents and educators to invest time and money for little or no gain. There is no one program or therapy I would endorse. Your journey may involve a behavioural optometrist or speech pathologist or other specialist. My only advice is to be wary of any program offering a quick solution. Continually ask questions, surround yourself with professionals in the field and work in conjunction with the school wherever possible.

This is one chapter in particular where I must absolutely lean on the stories and advice of others. When you know you are not an expert in an area you must call in the expert help.

Educator Tracey Hand of Optimise Learning has many years of experience in the classroom and in working one-on-one with young people to reach their potential. Here she outlines some common literacy issues and ways the reader can be supported. As always, each young person is different and must be treated as such with an individual plan that meets their particular needs.

Tracey Hand

In Australia, the term 'learning difficulty' is used to refer to students who experience significant difficulties in learning and making progress in school.[1]

Unfortunately, learning to read can be difficult for so many. As a classroom teacher I have had the privilege of teaching hundreds of young students how to read. During that time I often found myself wondering why some children learned to read quickly and seemingly effortlessly while others found it extremely difficult.

While my subsequent specialised training provided many insights into why this might be so, the main benefit of further study was the understanding

I developed in relation to the specific elements involved in the process of reading. This, combined with the knowledge of which particular teaching strategy to use and when, has enabled me to effectively assist students who experience difficulties with reading.

It is exciting to learn that recent advances in technology have enabled neuroscientists to view and study the brains of children as they are reading. This has led to a range of new understandings of how the brain learns to read, including:

- When a child is learning how to read they use different areas of the brain compared to a child who is an experienced and capable reader.
- Students who have difficulties with reading use a different area of the brain when decoding words than capable readers do.
- There is significantly more activity observed in the brain of a student with reading difficulties during reading. This indicates that the brain of a child with reading difficulties is working a lot harder than a student who finds reading easy.[2]

Observations of students' brains while they are reading has led to the understanding that, unlike speaking, the brain has no area specialised for reading. Speaking is considered to be an innate activity for the human brain whereas reading is not, which is why children need to be specifically taught how to read.

Learning to read can be challenging for many children, particularly for those who have a diagnosed learning difficulty, a few of which I'll explore in more detail here.

Dyslexia

Dyslexia has been defined by the International Dyslexia Association as: 'a specific learning disability that is neurological in origin. It is characterised by difficulties with accurate and/or fluent word recognition, decoding and by poor spelling'.[3]

Many children who have been diagnosed as having dyslexia may be considered by others to be reluctant readers, due to the difficulties they experience, and sadly some dyslexic students may come to view themselves in this way.

While learning the mechanics of reading is much more difficult for students with dyslexia, once they have learned how to read they can read to learn, which opens up a whole new world for them. Often students with dyslexia are highly creative and great problem solvers, meaning that 'story' – in whatever form that is accessed – will be something they will connect with.

To achieve optimal outcomes for dyslexic students it is vitally important for parents to seek specialised advice and support for their child. There are a wide range of support options and resources available for students with dyslexia and their parents. It is also imperative for parents to regularly communicate with their child's teacher and school, and support their child as needed with homework tasks and other areas of education.

Parents of dyslexic children can assist their child to develop a love of reading by continuing to read stories and books aloud to them regularly, even when their child has developed the ability to read independently. Students with dyslexia may always need to put more effort into their reading, so it is a good idea for parents to offer to read alternate pages of a book, or to access audio books, ebooks and graphic novels to enhance their child's reading experience and ensure access to the joy of stories.

Asking children with dyslexia to select books they would like to read or have read to them and then intentionally discussing the events in a story with them will assist children to view themselves as readers while giving them the opportunity to engage with and enjoy a wide variety of books.

Auditory processing disorder

Auditory processing disorder (APD) describes the inability to process the meaning of sound.[4]

Children who have been diagnosed with APD find it difficult to recognise the subtle differences between sounds, which can have a negative impact on their reading development if left untreated.

There are many support options and resources available to students with APD and it is very important for parents to organise specialised and ongoing support for their child as soon as a diagnosis of APD has been confirmed. Communicating regularly with their child's teacher and school is another routine parents of students diagnosed with APD should implement.

To support their child at home parents can reduce background noise wherever possible. They should speak slowly and intentionally to their child, giving no more than two directions at one time, and write lists or notes for their child to reference. Focusing on and reminding students of what they are capable of will assist them to develop their self-confidence and a positive attitude towards reading and learning.

Attentional issues

Learning and attention difficulties can affect a child's ability to focus. The learning difficulty most commonly linked to attentional problems is attention deficit hyperactivity disorder (ADHD). It is imperative for parents of children who have difficulty focusing and maintaining concentration to communicate regularly with their child's teacher and school. There are specific strategies and routines that can assist and support students with attentional difficulties. By keeping in close contact, teachers and parents can discuss the strategies and routines they have identified as being the most supportive for the child concerned and these can be implemented at home and at school.

Parents of children who have attentional difficulties can support their child's reading development at home by including reading as part of the daily routine. Sharing a book or reading aloud to their child just before bed each night can help them to relax before going to sleep. Writing letters and/or sight words on cards and using these to play memory, snap or other games can be useful for assisting children to develop their phonological awareness and vocabulary knowledge in ways that are more active than just reading lists of letters or sight words.

Helping their child to focus on one activity at a time and encouraging them to stop and listen when they are speaking to their child are other strategies parents can use to assist their child to focus and maintain concentration. It is vitally important for parents to seek specialised advice and support for their child if they feel concerned about their child's ability to focus or manage their impulsivity.

Visual problems

Research reveals that approximately 80% of information that is processed by the human brain is received via the visual system. Students who have visual problems risk compromising their reading development significantly if they do not have access to the specialised resources and support they require. Young students with visual problems who are learning how to read may not be able to recall different letters or numbers. Their ability to focus on print for long periods may also be reduced, which makes it difficult for them to develop efficient reading stamina, fluency and phrasing.

If a student with visual problems sees words on a page as blurry or double, they need to work hard at seeing the letters clearly, which can impact negatively on their enjoyment of reading and their comprehension skills. Because students with visual problems spend the majority of their time looking closely at letters and the words they form as they read, they often have difficulty tracking the lines of text, which can result in them missing lines. Using their finger to track text can be helpful, however doing so can lead to the habit of voice pointing, which prevents the skills of fluency and phrasing from being developed.

Research shows that when a visual problem has been diagnosed and corrected, most students develop a love for reading.

I also don't believe that any discussion of reading challenges should be without the perspectives of both a parent and a child who has experienced difficulty in learning to read. For many years I watched the journey of one particular student and marvelled at the tenacity and devotion of this mother in ensuring her daughter became a reader and knew the joy of story. I often observed her frustration but I also observed a quiet determination. For many years I both silently cheered her on from the sidelines and provided all the support I could to her daughter in my role as teacher librarian. I have asked her to share her story.

Raising a 'left-handed' learner reader

My husband and I did all the 'right' activities to help raise a reader and instil a love of literature in our daughter. Stories were read to her daily from the first few months of life; we both read a variety of materials ourselves; we live in house filled with books; she has her own extensive book collection; we displayed learning charts throughout our house; we sang and pointed to the alphabet song every night before bed and many times throughout the day. You name it, we tried it!

The kindergarten teacher once shared that our daughter always looked at situations, problems, etc, from a unique perspective, differently from most of her classmates. What I now know is that the kindergarten teacher was identifying a left-handed learning style without naming any of the components.

When my daughter was four I initiated an assessment by a speech and language pathologist as I knew something wasn't 'right'. This professional referred us to an occupational therapist and we started therapy for a period of time. Commencing school taught us both to dislike grading of readers (known as reading levels) with an intensity that is hard to articulate politely! From my perspective as a mother of a child with learning difficulties, sight words are the devil in disguise. I'm ashamed to share that there were far too many tears shed and tantrums (plus books) thrown by both child and parent as my daughter tried her best to learn to read. It was a genuinely heartbreaking nightmare. She was also bullied by her peers as she struggled to learn to read.

We had our daughter assessed by no less than five speech therapy services before we met our angel in disguise, a specialist in dyslexia. She diagnosed our daughter's learning style as dyslexia and introduced us to evidence-based interventions delivered with the degree of knowledge, skill, love and compassion possessed by the very best kind of allied health professionals. We worked very hard and our daughter has reaped the rewards of this hard work.

In addition to working with a specialist, we moved our daughter to a different school environment, spent a small fortune on audio books, iBooks and graphic novels, and we kept reading, reading, reading.

This is what I have learnt from my daughter's journey:

- Never, ever give up! Be your child's champion and advocate. If you don't or won't believe in your child, no one else – including themselves – ever will.
- Reading is about understanding. How we access the words, sentences and meaning is less important than the access itself. Eye (conventional), ear (audio) and finger (braille) reading are all equally valid and all involve the brain.
- Do the hard yards as soon as possible. Your child will reap the rewards later on. As my elder sister told me on many occasions you have to have thick, tough skin to be a parent. I made my daughter do many activities on her journey to being able to read independently that she wasn't thrilled about.
- Being able to spell doesn't make you a superior human being. It's just spelling, people, get over it! As my husband says, 'That's why we have spellcheck.'

If I had to nominate two interventions that were critical to our daughter becoming an independent reader who loves books they would be:

1. Finding the right allied health professional who works in the area. We will go to our graves forever loving the specialist we met and all her goodness.
2. Being in a supportive educational setting. Perfect doesn't exist in a school but find the best you can.

My beautiful, brave 'Dyslexian' (how my daughter describes herself) gave me the proudest parent moment when she 'ear' read (that is, listened to an audio book) Jane Austen's *Pride and Prejudice*. She read this book at the recommendation of a very high achieving academic superstar peer. I – who loved and excelled in English at school – confess to never having read a Jane Austen book. My heart burst with pride.

This story puts the human heart into what can be a tiring journey. We know that academic success is tied to reading and we, as parents, want our children to achieve their full potential. What I think this story shows is that full potential is reached when parents, educators and specialists work in partnership and the child is valued for the learner they are, and their strengths are both acknowledged and rewarded. It also shows that sometimes tough decisions need to be made in the best interests of the child. The next story is of a student (whom I'll call Abby) I taught for many years, and is similar in that the input of specialists, teachers and parents has been key in Abby reaching her full potential as a reader and learner. I interviewed Abby, with parental permission, for the story that follows.

I first met Abby as a Year One student. She had just changed schools due to the previous one not meeting her needs, mostly in the area of literacy. I had been told before her enrolment that Abby was absolutely terrified of the library as her experience of a school library to date had not been positive. The day she came to her first library lesson with me I curbed my usually over-the-top loud style of welcome and bent down to her level to introduce myself. She didn't want to come into the library that day so one of my staff took a few books out to her and together they sat outside to read.

It took some weeks before Abby was comfortable enough to enter the library and many months before she would talk to me and trust me. I was aware she was sizing me up and working out my style and

I did eventually win over this clever and sceptical little person. I am proud to say that, to this day, we are the best of teacher/student mates.

Throughout her early years of primary school, Abby worked hard at learning to read but it was often an exercise that reduced her to tears and heightened her anxiety around written work, assessments and library lessons. In Year Two she was diagnosed with dyslexia and received support and modifications to her learning and assessment as well as time with specialist staff, but reading and written work were very much things she 'didn't enjoy at all'. Throughout these years she was always comfortable in the library and when I asked her what she liked about our library, despite all the books (she had previously declared, 'Oh there are just *too many* books in this place! They freak me out!'), she said that it was because we 'didn't just do books in the library'.

Thanks to #bestteachingpartnerever Jackie Child, we had a great makerspace zone and vibe to our library. Abby was highly creative and loved to make and problem solve – the key skills embraced by the makerspace movement. For many years, Abby spent every lunchtime in the library creating wondrous objects out of paper, wood, fabric and glue or GoldieBlox and propellors. Her interest in motors and propellors lead her to create some great projects such as Scribble Bots. She was a highly valued member of the coding and robotics club and respected by her peers, who could see how creatively gifted she was and who were always keen to 'do the reading and writing bits for her' (her words).

The makerspace opened our library doors wide, welcoming everyone, including students who did not previously see themselves as 'library kids'. Our hope has always been that having spent time in the library making and creating, they will walk out with books. Abby regularly left the library with a book after a session in the makerspace, thanks in part to our placement of book displays on the way to and from the makerspace zone. As teacher librarians we also initiate regular conversations with students about books that might further their interests in a particular area. One day I could see Abby working on a robotic horse and armed her with several non-fiction books on horses so she could ensure hers was anatomically correct, as well as a fictional story about ponies I knew she would be able to read and enjoy.

Reading continued to be an immense challenge for Abby but she was an incredible storyteller who would write and illustrate lengthy narratives and share them with her friends and teachers who were adept at reading her phonetic spelling. When Readers' Cup competitions were held in school, Abby said she would be upfront about the fact that she was not going to understand or even read all of the books but that she would make up for it with her ability to 'think outside the box'. She was always a valued member of any Readers' Cup team.

Abby confessed that she often borrowed library books she never read (sweetpea, I already knew that!) so it looked like she was keeping up with her peers. But she did enjoy audio books and non-fiction texts and I would always slip a graphic novel into her pile of borrowing or maybe a novel I knew she would be able to read independently. There was regular communication between her parents and me about Abby's reading and what she would enjoy, so we made a great team!

Abby and her mother joined my Year Six Girl Zone Book Club. The set books were at a much higher reading level than what Abby could manage on her own, but the lovely thing about this book club is that I encourage parents or caregivers to read with or to their child and talk about the story as they go. I believe the book club was essential in making Abby confirm her identity as a reader – she was hanging out with 'the readers' so she must be a reader too, right?

Abby loves reading and while she still finds it difficult and experiences anxiety, she has a 'give it a go' attitude. Parents and educators have worked alongside her to ensure her success. But to be honest? Most of Abby's success is down to the hard work she has put in and her awareness that she loved stories very much so she was determined to access them any way she could.

Like Abby, many young people with reading or learning challenges discover the power of story through graphic novels. Allison Rushby is the award-winning author of several middle-grade novels and adult titles and she is also an avid reader of graphic novels. I suspect there are few, if any, households with a graphic novel collection quite like hers. I have asked her to talk about why and how she uses graphic novels, as well as her all-time favourite ten.

Allison Rushby

I grew up in a house of readers. As the daughter of a novelist and being a novelist myself, I simply expected my kids would be readers as well. It was clear from very early on that our firstborn, Ivy, was going to have some challenges in life. She was soon diagnosed as having a developmental delay that included a comprehension disorder. Her presentation is unusual and it often takes educators quite some time to understand her learning style. Ivy has good spelling and reading but poor comprehension. Her good spelling and reading stem from her enhanced visual skills, which she has developed because she relies on visual cues to get by in the world. Because her comprehension is poor, standard print novels are confusing for her. Audio books can be a useful tool for people with learning difficulties, but because a comprehension disorder is all-encompassing, audio books are also not much use to us (in fact, they are even harder for Ivy to comprehend as there are no visual cues at all).

I knew that if I wanted Ivy to read and enjoy books, graphic novels were really going to be our only option. I needed to become knowledgeable about them. And fast. So I did. I am constantly on the hunt, ordering in from overseas, looking for what's out in which territories, what's coming out soon and often pre-ordering a year in advance. I think we got very lucky with our timing. In recent years graphic novels have taken off in a big way. In fact, graphic novels are now so popular that Scholastic has developed an entire imprint around them (called Graphix).

I'm constantly surprised at the snobbery that persists around graphic novels – I often hear parents saying things like, 'Oh, but I want my child to read a real novel.' To be honest I doubt whether this will continue much longer. With graphic novels constantly on *The New York Times* bestseller list, they can no longer be overlooked.

Megan has asked that I submit my top ten graphic novels and I'm ashamed to say I'm going to cheat disgracefully and include series and more than one book per entry. But your child's love of reading will only be enhanced for it so I'm really not that ashamed at all! Although not top favourites, I have included a few examples of books you will often find on the curriculum that are available in graphic novel form as I often find parents aren't aware of their existence and they do make authors like Shakespeare far more accessible.

1. *Smile* and *Sisters* by Raina Telgemeier
2. The Amulet series by Kazu Kibuishi
3. *El Deafo* by Cece Bell
4. *A Midsummer Night's Dream* the graphic novel in plain text by William Shakespeare (*Romeo and Juliet, Macbeth* and others are also available)
5. The Baby-Sitter's Club graphic novel collection based on the novels of Ann M. Martin, illustrated by Raina Telgemeier and Gale Galligan
6. Percy Jackson & The Olympians graphic novel series by Rick Riordan, adapted by Robert Venditti
7. *Awkward* by Svetlana Chmakova
8. *Roller Girl* by Victoria Jamieson
9. *Anne of Green Gables* the graphic novel by Lucy Maud Montgomery, adapted by Mariah Marsden, illustrated by Brenna Thummler
10. *Jane Eyre* the graphic novel by Charlotte Bronte, adapted by Amy Corzine, illustrated by John M. Burns

THE GENDER DEBATE

I have worked in both co-ed and single-sex schools and I've heard the gamut of thoughts on 'gendered' books. When I worked as a teacher librarian in a boys' school, I had so many people commenting along the lines of, 'Well, you'll have a hard time getting boys reading!' I found this both infuriating and disappointing and would have loved to have shown these naysayers my library on any given lunch break, filled with young male readers. To be fair, some of those boys were there for the chess, to look at surfing magazines or use the iPads, but they were comfortable in a space of books, and borrowing rates were high. Some of the best conversations about books I ever had were in that library and the requests for new books came in thick and fast. I now work in an all-girls school library and I have similar rate of borrowing and the same sorts of conversations around books. The book choices on the shelves are also largely the same; although I'll admit that shark and train books were more prevalent in the boys' school library, and hairstyle and fairy books do dominate in the girls' school. But I always aim to stock my library with books that will appeal to all and the general fiction collection I have had in both co-ed and single-sex schools has always looked similar.

We can do our young readers a disservice by making assumptions about what boys will read and what girls will read. I see and acknowledge the differences in bookish taste, but I also see similarities in what all readers will access and enjoy if given the opportunity.

Jacqueline Harvey is one of Australia's most popular authors for children (Alice-Miranda, Clementine Rose, and Kensy and Max series) and a highly experienced teacher and presenter of talks and workshops at schools and festivals around the world. We have had discussions about book gendering time and time again. Jacqueline has much to say about why the labelling has to stop.

Jacqueline Harvey

If I had a dollar for every time I've heard a parent (or teacher) actively steer their boy away from reading one of my books, sadly I'd have enough money to keep me in expensive coffee for quite some time. It happens at book signings (when the child has clearly been keen to meet me), it happens at schools – it just happens. 'You don't want that, it's got a girl on the cover'; 'Maaate, that's a book for girls'; 'Boys don't read those books' – you get the picture. And I know I'm not alone. I've had this discussion with many of my author friends who write books with girls as the central characters.

As a former teacher I know it doesn't take a huge amount of encouragement to convince a girl to pick up a book with a boy on the cover, but try that in reverse and more often than not it's an insurmountable challenge. If we're not encouraging our boys to read books with girls as the main characters we're doing them a great disservice. What are we telling our boys? That stories about girls are lesser – they don't matter as much – they're not as good as boys? And never mind that many books with girls on the cover include boy characters in the stories – I know mine have loads of them.

Even worse is when during school visits I've been confronted in a co-ed school by a room full of girls. When I've asked where the boys are I've been met with, 'Well, you know, we didn't think they'd enjoy your talk because your books are for girls.' At which point my head is about to explode. I pride myself on being able to entertain and inform all children in my talks – my talks are fun and fabulous and I've had lots of feedback that confirms I'm good at this. To think that boys miss out because the teacher (who in all likelihood hasn't even read my books) has decided that I only write books for girls is not only ludicrous but offensive to me – an educator with over twenty years' experience. I cannot imagine the girls being removed from a talk by a male author who writes about male protagonists – it just wouldn't happen.

Okay, the publishers play a big role in perpetuating the myths. Marketing is often quite gender specific. Books with sparkly, pink rainbow unicorns on the cover probably won't appeal as much to boys as to girls, and I get that boys and girls lean towards different things. But just a girl – a girl who looks like she's going to have an adventure and probably bring down a bad guy or two – why is that still a problem, even if the background cover is purple or, heaven forbid, pink? My covers have a whole palette of colours from blue to green to yellow and inky black as well as pink and purple. Society has come a long way but to think that the gatekeepers still limit the reading choices of our boys by reinforcing gender stereotypes is disappointing to say the least.

I write about strong girls (and boys). They have adventures, they solve mysteries, they're funny and clever and kooky. They travel to different countries and learn new things, they have fun, yet my audience is still probably around 95 per cent female. When I do meet my boy readers they are passionate. I love asking them why they like Alice-Miranda or Clementine Rose. Here are some of the responses: 'I don't like Alice-Miranda, I love her ...'; 'She feels like my best friend ...'; 'She's brave and funny and she has great adventures ...'; 'Clemmie has a pet pig and she's always getting herself into trouble ...'; 'I love the mysteries ...'

One of my favourite anecdotes about boy readers happened at a major Australian writers' festival a few years ago. I'm not going to name names but I was on the bill with three of the biggest (male) names in children's literature. During my last signing session three boys in Year Six approached me with books. Their librarian who was standing beside them said, 'Tell Jacqueline why you're buying her books.' I was intrigued. One of the boys explained that before they were allowed to come to the event they had to read a book by each of the authors and they all enjoyed mine the most. Did that make me feel awesome? You bet! I asked those boys to go back to school and share their love of Alice-Miranda with their friends. Who knows if they did but good for them for being brave enough to pick up a book with a girl on the cover and for admitting they enjoyed it.

Unfortunately those experiences are far too few – and not because I don't think boys will enjoy my books. I'm writing a new series with a boy and a girl on the cover. Kensy and Max are twins and they're about to find out something amazing about their family. Will boys read it because there is a boy on the cover? Who knows! But I hope so and I hope they might go back and explore some of my other stories too – once they know for sure that I don't just write books for girls!

KEEPING TWEENS READING

Life commonly gets busy with homework and after-school activities for kids once they hit middle/upper primary school. A report commissioned by the State Library of Victoria's Centre For Youth Literature (CYL) examining the Australian reading landscape found that as students move from primary to secondary school, reading for pleasure declines and even previously keen readers often disengage from literature.[5] The pressure is on to help young people find a balance between reading, social media, socialising, studying and extra-curricular pursuits.

It is also a challenging age in terms of book choices as they begin to transition from younger reader books to middle-grade novels and young adult (YA) books. I have plenty of senior primary students at school who get all angsty at my lack of 'adult content' books, but then I also have many who are still happy reading tales about fairies and puppies. I see a huge range of reading maturity and it keeps me on my toes catering for the wide variety of reading ages and stages. As always, conversations with individual children and their parents are the key to success here.

If you feel your child is needing or wanting to make the transition to middle-grade novels, I would encourage you to read alongside them for a while to ensure the process is smooth. As a bonus, I guarantee that you will enjoy many of the middle-grade novels, as much as your child does. Middle-grade is a description of a reading demographic, not a genre type, with these novels being targeted at students in the upper years of primary school and early years of secondary school. They typically clock in at around 40,000 to 50,000 words in length. Tweens are emerging from their childhood years and becoming more aware that the world is a large and sometimes scary place. For this reason, middle-grade novels often feature themes of friendships, family, social issues and community or wider world issues, with relatable central characters who navigate complex situations and try to solve problems. It is common for children to want to read novels with characters who are the same age or slightly older, using the experiences, mistakes and successes of the characters to question how they might face similar realities in their own lives. Tweens and teens want independence and the space to take risks, but also want to receive reassurance both in real life and in their reading choices. Through the vicarious experience offered by reading novels, they have the opportunity to step into other people's shoes and walk with them, developing empathy and understanding.

I overheard a conversation some years ago in my library that has always stayed with me. It was between two eleven-year-olds and one was recommending the other a beautiful middle-grade novel called *Mother's Day* (Anne Brooksbank) saying, 'I think you should read this book. It's got a divorced family and the main character is trying to work out what is happening with her mum. It's a little bit like what happened to Maggie's family and I actually feel like I kind of was in Maggie's head when I was reading it.' I had to walk away because (a) I had tears in my eyes at how amazing this level of bookish understanding was and (b) these students were sharing a special moment and I was not going to step in and ruin it.

Chapter 14, 'Reading the Dark', gives further insights, but the tween years are also the time when parents and educators will notice a distinct shift in the themes explored in literature. Children are more aware of some of the darker themes in life, and literature is often where they will explore the moral and ethical issues around challenging topics. Literature can be a gateway to some really tough conversations, at an age where conversation with adults is often at a minimum. Talking through book characters has certainly been something I have done with my ten-year-old when trying to talk about the grief and loss we have experienced as a family. Feeding her a book every now and then with a bereaved character has meant we can talk about the character, rather than her own feelings, something she is not yet willing or able to do. At all times it is imperative to balance the light and the dark in the literature your tweens are reading, but try to not be alarmed by books with darker themes. Quality middle-grade novels manage the big emotions with care: deep friendships but little or no romance; minimal or no violence; depression with hope; grief with moments of light and laughter. On writing middle-grade novels, author Allison Tait states, 'Basically, you don't want to traumatise your readers. You want to evoke emotion and provoke thought, but you have to remember that your ideal reader is a child.'[6]

If you find yourself with a tween or classful of them who have stalled with their reading, I would recommend trying some of the following ideas:

- Sign them up to an online reading challenge like the MS Readathon or the Premier's Reading Challenges in your state – there is nothing like a bit of pressure to read and the lure of a certificate and/or prizes.
- Offer new books as a reward for tasks done or as end-of-school or end-of-term gifts.
- Read with them. Middle-grade novels are as fabulous for adults as they are for children (think of the success of Harry Potter in the adult market). This comes back to what I have said earlier about being a reading role model, but it also shows your tween or teen that you value the books they read. It also means you will be present when spontaneous conversations about issues start to flow.

- Read to them. Reading the first chapter or two of a really great middle-grade novel will often pique enough interest for them to pick up the book left lying around.
- Browse blogs, author social media accounts and popular tween magazines, and let your child choose their reading material – a sense of independence is all important. Autonomy in reading choices is crucial at this age, but that autonomy can and often should be guided by a parent or teacher.
- Attend book launches, local library events, children's literature festivals and bookshops. There is nothing like meeting an author to inspire reading, and middle-grade authors are some of the coolest people you and your tweens will ever meet.
- Join a book club! I run a book club at my school for eleven-year-old girls and their mum, grandma, aunt or older sister. For many of my participants it's their favourite co-curricular activity and parents have commented that it's been such a good way to bond with their child at what can be a tricky time to remain really connected. See 'How to start a book club' (page 223) for hints.

Some of these ideas might seem forced, even onerous, but if your child connects with some books they adore then they will be off and flying with their reading again.

I have asked one of my favourite teen readers, Joe Visser (AKA Book Boy), to talk about his teen reading journey. His reviews have appeared in *The Sunday Telegraph* and on sites such as *Children's Books Daily* and *Creative Kids Tales*. You can check out his blog at www.bookboy.com.au.

Joe Visser (AKA Book Boy)

I've always read widely, including books that I may not be the target audience for, be it books for girls, or books that are sometimes considered 'too old' for someone my age. But reading these books, I believe, furthers a young person's understanding of the world.

The first book I can remember reading by myself was the second Harry Potter book. I read the first one with Mum when I was five or six, and that kind of sparked my love of reading. My mum has been very influential in the kinds of books I read – she recommends a lot of books to me – but more recently, I have heard about books through other people or mediums.

I listen to the *Dear Hank and John* podcast, which has influenced what I read a lot lately, especially in regard to poetry (I've been reading a lot more of it). I also hear about books through friends, and my English teachers have given me some suggestions.

Teenagers, especially boys, generally stop reading or read less when they turn fourteen or fifteen. There are a few possible reasons for this. Often it is around this age that you start to read and analyse books for school so there is less time to read for enjoyment.

Another reason is that young people may wish to start reading more 'grown-up' books and their parents may not let them. I think this is a mistake. I'm not saying that parents should let their children read whatever they want as there is some material in books that is not appropriate to expose a young person to, but I suggest that parents read the book first, and think about how bad it would really be to let their child read it.

When I turned thirteen I started reading more books that were considered to be for adults, from authors such as Stephen King and books such as *All the Light We Cannot See* by Anthony Doerr. Because my mother had read these before, she knew what they were about and that they posed little or no threat if I were to read them. Books such as *A Game of Thrones* by George R. R. Martin are ones I am not allowed to read yet.

I also read books that are 'for girls' or aimed at girls (or books with girl protagonists) because a good book is a good book, no matter who the target audience is.

Another teen book blogger to keep an eye on is Jazzy of *Jazzy's Bookshelf*. She is an MS Readathon ambassador and writes insightful reviews and articles about her teen reading journey.

SUPPORTING THE MOVE INTO YA READING

Young adult (YA) books are aimed at readers from around the age of thirteen plus, but there is wide variance within the genre. Some are exclusively aimed at readers sixteen plus, so it is important to look at the suitability of each book for your own young readers. YA literature has always been popular but perhaps the rise in social media has meant it has more of a presence because young people are the biggest consumers and creators of social media content. The YA literature scene has kept up with this and embraced the trend with enthusiasm (the hashtag #LoveOzYA is a great one to follow).

Like middle-grade, YA is a reading demographic, not a genre, so there are many types of stories exploring a range of topics and styles. Teens are able to find something they like amid sub-genres and series and accompanying online communities. There have always been teenagers who read and share passionately and the growth in social media has made it easier to connect with other passionate readers. Fan-fiction writing and artwork have found spaces in Tumblr and DeviantArt. With the plethora of online book communities (Goodreads, listy, BookLikes and Riffle books), the opportunities to be validated by others has amplified the interest in YA books.

YA books are popular with both teens and adults because they are relatable and appeal to a wide and diverse audience. Many adults actually prefer reading YA novels to lengthier adult tomes. Authors of quality YA are skilled writers who remove every extraneous word, leaving only the very best and essential, and the true beating heart of the story: all the emotion and tension of an adult novel but punchier and more to the point. YA authors are often risk-takers (as are their readers!) and don't feel obligated to stick to a formula, often meshing genres together. They often also touch on profoundly important topics such as homelessness (*Because of You* by Pip Harry), the plight of refugees (*The Bone Sparrow* by Zana Fraillon), identity (*Take Three Girls* by Cath Crowley, Simmone Howell and Fiona Wood), sexuality (*The Sidekicks* by Will Kostakis), grief (*The Protected* by Claire Zorn), and LGBTQIA acceptance (*You Know Me Well* by David Levithan and Nina LaCour). There has been a strong call for more diverse and #ownvoices, so that authors like Will Kostakis, Randa Abdel-Fattah and Benjamin Alire Saenz are given space to bring more marginalised and distinct voices to life.

In recent years filmmakers have latched on series such as The Hunger Games (Suzanne Collins) and realised how much good YA there is to exploit. It can often be much easier to sell a book to a reluctant reader when there is also a film. Librarians also capitalise on movie tie-ins and while it seems like movies would draw kids away from reading, both mediums benefit the other. I am a massive fan of the YA-book-to-movie phenomenon and have seen just about every incarnation of them over the last ten years – you'll often find keen teacher librarians up the back of the cinema of teen 'book-to-movie' releases.

CHAPTER SEVEN

THE SOCIAL LIFE OF YOUNG READERS

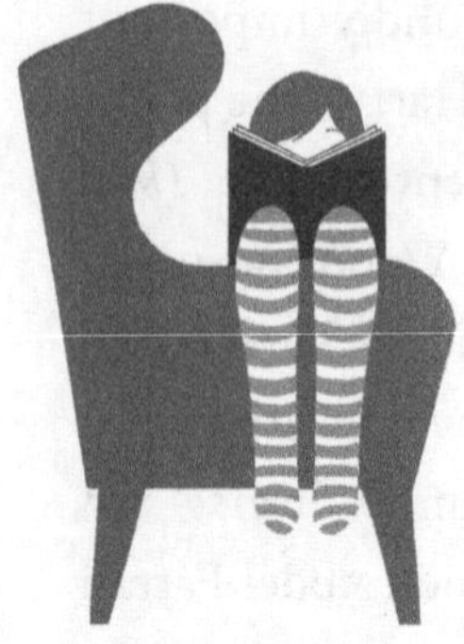

Reading is generally considered a solitary pursuit. Sitting alone in one's personal home library with a cup of tea and a slice of cake on a plate resting on the arm of the plush green velvet reading chair with the perfect pendant light illuminating the pages of a new novel. Well, this is one of my fantasies anyway. When we imagine readers we picture them alone. Popular media has a tendency to portray 'the reader' negatively and it does reading such a disservice.

Being a librarian draws next-level media stereotyping. I recently got reading glasses for the first time and the full-bearded, waistcoat-wearing hipster optometrist got so excited when he found out I was a librarian. 'Oh my! Imagine being a legit librarian now with your brown cardigans, brogues and glasses.' It wasn't really the look I was going for.

My younger brother, who has just come through his own man-bun, bearded hipster phase, certainly doesn't fit the stereotype of 'the reader'. He is a mad keen surfer, used to be a builder, now works in finance, can hold his own in any social situation – and is a voracious reader. He wasn't a reader as a child and my parents despaired. But on a very boring work trip to Paris with my parents during his early teens he discovered Harry Potter, and has never looked back.

Readers come in all shapes, sizes and persuasions and the world of reading can be a ridiculously social place. Still, stereotypes exist for a reason and many readers are happy to embrace the solitary reader tag and wear it with pride. I just hope that readers can also be seen as vibrant, highly sociable and excellent conversationalists.

COMPETITIONS FOR READERS

Book-based competitions are the time for readers to shine! A Readers' Cup-style competition is a way to have students participate in meaningful and wide reading. I liken Readers' Cup to a sporting activity: there are teams to form; training and preparation to do; competitions to fight, and much socialising and solidifying of friendships in 'downtime'. In fact, I wonder if some teams even *read* the books as so much time seems to be spent chatting and laughing and gossiping about other teams. Readers' Cup competitions sometimes even support the creation of uniforms. PudStar was once in a team called the 'Reading Ninjas' so they all wore black, had ninja bands and paper ninja stars.

Readers' Cup competitions consist of teams of four students who read from a list of approximately six books chosen for their particular competition, be it school, regional or state based. Team members are encouraged to read all books on their list and 'train' together by discussing the books and asking practice questions with each other. In many states of Australia there will be school heats in Term One with the winning team going on to the regional heats in Term Two, and the state finals held in Term Three. Readers' Cup began in South Australia and exists across Australia, though not all states yet run regional and state heats.

If you do not have a Readers' Cup or similar competition in your

FIVE WAYS TO ENSURE YOU PRODUCE AN EVER-SO-SOCIABLE READER

1. Advocate for author visits in your school community and ensure the build-up is akin to a rock star visit. Author visits are fun, shared experiences and break down negative stereotypes about 'those who read books'.
2. Sign up to the email lists and social media accounts of local bookshops and festivals and look out for literary events. There are teen book clubs run by bookshops and festivals, story times for younger ones and craft and writing workshops for all ages. These events attract like-minded parents and children, and I often find the same faces at events around town.
3. Consider your local public library as your friend. My own children are booked into many library activities and they love them. We often take friends along or they will settle in and make some new friends over a two-hour gardening workshop or a mini-party to celebrate the birthday of a book.
4. Join a book club for young people with your child or sign them up to an age-appropriate one. If your school library doesn't have a book club, start one with friends and their children or find one at your local independent bookshop or public library.
5. Follow authors on social media and connect with other readers in the same way. Obviously I'm not advocating for young people on social media, but for teens this has become a way for them to connect with like-minded souls the world over. There are all kinds of reading and writing groups for people to join online and it's amazing how many authors hang out on social media and love to connect with their readers.

school community and would like to start one up, it's important to first gain the support of your principal and other teaching staff. A Readers' Cup competition can be a great learning opportunity, but if a class already has a heavy reading load, teachers will have a hard time encouraging students to read another five books. We now have our interschool Readers' Cup in Term Three as this forms part of our Book Week celebrations and we often choose a shortlisted book as one of the titles to be read. In other schools, set classroom texts are sometimes used as one of the Readers' Cup titles or teachers will read one text aloud to their class.

AUTHOR VISITS

Never underestimate the power of author or illustrator visits in schools, kindergartens or public libraries to inspire students and staff. Meeting the creators of books makes the writing and/or illustrating process accessible and can inspire students with their own creative projects.[1] Author and illustrator visits provide unique insights into the process of book creation and bring literature to life for students, giving them a rich understanding of the literary and artistic devices employed by an author or illustrator to construct meaning.

School libraries have shrinking budgets that are often spent on library resources, with author visits seen as the 'icing on the cake' only if money allows. It would be easy to assume that I speak from a position of privilege as all of the schools I have worked at over the last twenty years have allowed me to fund paid author visits and have been enthusiastic and grateful for free promotional visits. However, in each school, my library team and I have worked hard to ensure the school community understands the value of school author visits.

Author visits are possible in schools of any size and economic sway. It is a matter of advocating, fundraising and working towards your author visit goals. It is so very easy to put author visits in the too-hard basket or justify the lack of them due to poor funding or interest from school management. Being glum about a lack of funding or interest is never going to magic up an author visit, but being an enthusiastic advocate will.

Free author visits: promote, promote, promote!

Where funds are limited, schools can take up offers of free visits from local authors or illustrators who are keen to build their audience and promote their work. Occasionally publishers or bookstores will offer free school visits as part of a promotional tour or by arrangement with a charity such as the Dymocks Children's Charity. Promotion of the author and their books is expected for free visits, and I make sure that I send home promotional flyers and book order forms before the talk. The aim of the author, bookstore or publisher with free visits is to sell copies of books and increase awareness about an author or book. Such visits are a win for all involved *if* the school does a thorough job of promoting the event, and teaching staff and school administration see the value. For these visits I do not expect the presenter to conduct workshops or in-depth writing lessons that form part of the curriculum; rather I see these sessions as a way to build excitement and fanfare around books and reading within the school community.

Paid author visits: connect with curriculum!

Paid author visits are an entirely different matter and I budget for at least two paid author or illustrator visits each school year. I communicate with speakers agencies or consider my own contacts in the children's book industry to decide who would best meet the needs of the school community. In collaboration with teachers, I work out which areas of the curriculum might be most enhanced by working with or hearing from an author or illustrator. Involving

THE THRILL OF MEETING YOUR FAVOURITE AUTHOR OR ILLUSTRATOR

As I read PudStar her books tonight and she tried to keep her eyes open after a *massive* day at StoryArts Festival in Ipswich, she pondered her favourite illustrators. 'I think my second favourite illustrators are now Tony Flowers and Peter Carnavas because they were really good teachers today and Tony Flowers said it was okay to make your illustrations fart.' When I asked who her *favourite* illustrator was she looked at me incredulously: 'Me, of *course*!' How wonderful to think that these two generous illustrators inspired her to believe that she is also an illustrator.

Earlier in the day I had overheard her talking with her friend and listing the authors she had met at the festival and her friend asked in a hushed tone, 'What about Nikki Gemmell? Did you meet her?' to which PudStar replied, 'Well, she's not at this festival, but I'm meeting her *really* soon' and they both squealed, jumped and hugged. She's actually *not* meeting Nikki Gemmell anytime that I know of and perhaps I should discuss the importance of telling the truth, but it was very cool to witness young people discussing authors like famous pop stars.

teachers is crucial as they are best situated to facilitate many of the connections between author, students and curriculum. They play a key role in motivating and empowering students to apply the knowledge learned to their own reading and writing.[2]

For many years I invited Narelle Oliver to do storyboarding workshops with students in Year Three and lino-cutting workshops with Year Six. These workshops, held over several days, connected with several curriculum areas and provided real-life opportunities for students to engage with a masterful teacher, author and artist. Teachers were expected to complete prep work before the visit, which involved reading her books and completing an author study.

After the visit many weeks were spent following up on the work begun in workshops.

I was recently chatting with a Year Eleven student about a story she was writing for English and she pulled out of her bag a handmade concertina-fold book which was her story plan. She had learnt this technique of storyboarding in Year Three with Narelle Oliver and was still using it all these years later; these are the moments we live for as teachers. Over the years I have met a number of adults who vividly recall Narelle Oliver's workshops they participated in twenty years ago at primary school. Not every author visit will connect with every child, but there are moments of pure connection that last a lifetime for some students.

Author Kathryn Apel spent several days working with students from Year Three to Year Six on poetry writing last year. What the students learned was phenomenal! As an added bonus, staff came away just as inspired as the students and feeling far more confident in their ability to teach and create poetry. We have since added several of Kathryn Apel's verse novels to our set reading lists and I have seen many teachers incorporate exercises Kat shared with students into their poetry lessons. Kat Apel and I had communicated before the workshop to brainstorm ways to engage a range of teachers, some being maths teachers. Kat came up with a poetry workshop for the maths classes that incorporated the rules of Fibonacci numbers. This a great example of weaving language and story through *all* areas of the curriculum. For more information on author visits check out 'How to host an author or illustrator visit' (page 228) for tips on getting the most out of a visit to your school.

LITERARY AND BOOK-RELATED EVENTS

Some families go to sporting events, some travel to the beach or the bush each weekend, and some like to watch movies together. My family seems to lean towards literary events - probably something you can't escape when several members of the family are librarians. Literary pursuits, fuelled by excellent coffee for the adults, are what we *do* and some of our best family memories are of book launches and other bookish events around town.

In an age where our young people spend more and more time glued to screens, there is something a bit special and fabulous about a trip to your local library, bookstore, theatre or gallery to discover some reading gems and engage with creative activities. Literary events fire young minds and if a young person connects with the ideas presented in a workshop or production, they will be busy for days afterwards honing new skills. When books come to life in the form of a literary event, children fully immerse themselves in the story and experience it with all their senses.

Finding out about literary events

Pretty much every week I check in with the social media and email lists of my favourite local independent bookstores, council library, our state library and our magnificent art gallery to see what upcoming events they have planned. Many of these events are free or low cost; the hardest part is finding out about them and booking a spot.

Public libraries

Public libraries are simply the *best* places to visit with young people and they almost always have a fabulous calendar of free events.

Workshops are run by artists, authors, gardeners and performers and they are, without a doubt, some of the best my children and I have ever attended. They are creative, suit all ages and genders, and encourage engagement in community - wins all round, I say. With the recent focus on coding, makerspaces and robotics in libraries there are also a wide range of activities on these topics. Library workshops generally aim to 'increase engagement with the collection', so whether you have an avid reader or a reluctant reader, these workshops will always see you walking away with armfuls of borrowed books.

Bookstores

Bookstores have become extremely events-driven in the last five years or so and this has been a wonderful bonus for those of us who love nothing more than a great literary event. Even better is the fact that the best bookstores also have amazing coffee shops – I cannot understand why more parents have not cottoned on to the wonders of a Sunday morning bookshop trip: breakfast, multiple coffees, author workshops or signings, and some retail therapy. Our local bookstore has a dedicated children's bookstore next door and if I had all the time in the world I could book my children into an event most weeks. My friends and I also spend time at bookstore events in the evenings, enjoying a glass of wine, some cheese and a talk by our latest author love. Some bookstores host book clubs for young people, which are invaluable in connecting like-minded little souls.

State libraries

I am immensely fond of the various state libraries around Australia. We recently attended a brilliant community day where ChickPea sat entranced as all the instruments in the orchestra were introduced to her, PudStar had books read to her by one of the coolest authors around, Anita Heiss, and we all made family trees – which included our dogs, of course. We attended a fabulous 'create a character' workshop with author/illustrator Leigh Hobbs and spent several hours relaxing, reading, storytelling and crafting. And it was all free!

For older children, many of the state libraries run subsidised writing programs or digital media courses. There are so many young

MEETING AUTHORS AND ILLUSTRATORS IS AWESOME!

At a Jacqueline Harvey high tea event I once hosted, Jacqueline enthralled the audience with her talk and with her genuine warmth and enthusiasm. She spent several hours signing books and posters for young fans, her smile never once fading. PudStar's last words before bed that night were, 'She hugged me, Mummy! Jacqueline Harvey wrote Clementine Rose and she HUGGED me!' Never underestimate the impact a brilliant author visit can have on a child.

people out there who want to write, illustrate and meet the creators of books and these sorts of opportunities are priceless. Sign up to the email list of your state library as this contact is invaluable.

Theatre and live performance events

There is nothing better than a book or story transformed into a stage production, ballet, play-based experience, dance class, digital experience or visual art workshop. Literary outings extend the book reading experience, adding another dimension to the story and allowing young readers and young viewers to experience it in a different format. We attend many theatre productions that have a literary bent because they allow you to prepare young children by reading the book or telling the story, so that they will have a better idea of the narrative structure of the work before they attend.

There are fabulous theatre and ballet companies as well as festivals that are using books as the basis for their productions. We saw *The Peasant Prince*, a play based on the wonderful book of the same name by Li Cunxin and Anne Spudvilas (in book form there are adult, younger reader and picture book editions of the story). The adaptation of *The Peasant Prince* absolutely brought this book to life for myself and my children, and I spent much of the performance with goosebumps watching this amazing story leap from the pages onto the stage.

Author and illustrator workshops and festivals

It's wonderful being able to nicely stalk children's author/illustrator/publisher social media, blogs and websites. I have often been delighted to find that one of my favourite book creators is offering a holiday workshop or term-long art class. A few years ago some friends and I took a road trip to Murwillumbah with a group of seven-year-olds to do a day workshop illustrating, printing and creating books with talented children's book illustrator Tamsin Ainslie. It was the most fabulous day and much art was created by the little people. Literary day trips, with some coffee shop hopping and local gallery visiting for the adults, is the perfect outing for everyone involved.

Local authors will often schedule talks, workshops or meet-and-greets in local bookstores or libraries and of course at writers' festivals. My own children have grown up surrounded by literary types and have developed quirky little relationships with many of them. My eldest daughter will often re-read *Piccolo and Annabelle* (Stephen Axelsen), just because she loves Stephen Axelsen and recognises his voice and wry humour in his writing. Again, it is about finding a connection with books in whatever way works for you and your child.

BOOK CLUBS

I run a parent/child book club and this is my most favourite extra-curricular activity. Some teachers love nothing better than coaching soccer or blowing a whistle on a netball court, but my skills do not extend to such pursuits. I've pretty much been banned from involvement in school sport following some 'incidents' which are best left unmentioned but which did provide much laughter in the staffroom at my expense. Let's say no more! My book clubs are for *all* young people – those who adore reading and those who do not (and perhaps need a little nudge in the right direction or some guidance in what to read). Book clubs are simply about the joy of recreational reading and encouraging reading as a social activity. They help us to:

- Connect with others through a shared love of literature
- Discuss the big ideas and messages in literature
- Personally connect with a story or character.

If your school library doesn't have a book club but you would like your young reader to join one, start one up with friends and their children or find one at your local independent bookshop or public library. A book club can be as informal or formal as you choose. Make the decision based on the needs of your members, but remember that it is all about getting your readers enthusiastic about books – it is not a study group!

Some of the following questions and ideas are great to use as a starting point for guiding discussion. Do keep in mind that these are a guide only and will not suit each book you read. I have these printed out on laminated cards and small groups discuss several questions before reporting back to the whole book club group.

- Does the title 'fit' the book?
- Do the characters seem real and believable? To what extent do they remind you of yourself or someone you know?
- Is the focus on a single character or on several whose lives are intertwined?
- What is the point of view from which the story is told?
- Is the reader expected to identify with the characters or observe them?
- Think about the pacing. Are the characters and plot quickly revealed or slowly unveiled?

- Did any songs spring to mind as you read this book? As a group could you create a playlist to go with your book? See Claire Zorn's *One Would Think the Deep* for an example of a book playlist.
- Is there a linear plot or are there multiple plotlines, flashbacks or alternating chapters related from different points of view?
- Does the story emphasise people or does it highlight situations and events?
- What message do you think the author is trying to convey?
- What are the major themes of the book and do you feel they are relevant today?
- Does this book fit into or fight against a literary genre? How does the author use [science fiction, humour, tragedy, romance] to effect in the novel?
- How is humour (or other applicable emotion) explored in the language, ideas and characters of the books?
- Would this book make a good movie? Why?
- Who would you recommend this book to and why?
- Have you discovered anything about yourself as a reader as you read this book? Perhaps you've always avoided [insert the applicable genre] but found you really enjoyed this novel?

BOOK LAUNCHES

I have been taking my children to book launches from birth and they are often events you can happily take even very young children to – just be guided by the age range of the book as to what age child the launch may be aimed at. Book launches are mostly short events with 30 to 40 minutes' worth of formalities and a book reading before signings and festivities. Many authors will organise activities for young fans to be involved in, and there is often food, at least a celebratory cake, for hungry little people.

One of my favourite book launches remains the launch of Narelle Oliver's *Don't Let a Spoonbill in the Kitchen*. It was an afternoon of true book celebration and a riot of music, art activities, book buying and indulging in wonderful cupcakes that looked like they had leapt from the pages of the book. The then Governor-General of Australia, Quentin Bryce, launched the book and she spoke with immense warmth and sincerity about the power of books in the life of a child and the honour of being able to meet the creators of picture books. Narelle took the audience through the process of creating the rhyming text and the vibrant illustrations with many an anecdote thrown in about problems encountered along the way, all relayed with her self-deprecating drawl and twist of humour. This book launch was an affair to remember and many years later PudStar still takes *Don't Let a Spoonbill in the Kitchen* off the bookshelf and pores over the pages. For her this story now has a story *behind* it and will always hold a special place in her literary heart.

FIVE REASONS TO ATTEND CHILDREN'S BOOK LAUNCHES

1. To meet the authors and illustrators behind the books.
2. To celebrate the birth of another story with cake, clapping and much merriment.
3. For a little glimpse into how a book came to life.
4. For the ritual of a launch – listening to the various speakers, a lovely book reading and the signing and dedicating of books.
5. For the conversations that follow.

CHAPTER EIGHT

A BALANCED LITERARY DIET – A FEAST OF GENRES

Giving young people choice in what they read is crucial to them developing a love of reading. Teacher librarians and school libraries are all about free-choice reading. I've long been a vocal advocate for 'let them read what they want, when they want', including what I like to refer to as the 'marginalised genres' such as vampire stories, chick lit, horror, toilet humour and romance. However, I confess that, as a parent, I'm sometimes a little concerned by the reading choices my children make.

PudStar has been through a stage of reading only short, mass-produced books full of toilet humour. But when I say a 'stage', it went on for six months and she would read nothing else and could spot a toilet humour book from the front entrance of a bookstore or library. I'd be lying if I said I wasn't frustrated. I once added a 'worthy' text to her pile of fart books on the counter of our favourite local children's bookstore, mainly to cover said pile of fart books. Afterwards I gave myself a stern talking to about being grateful that my children were choosing to read and that the fart book phase would pass. It did, although she still loves a good poo joke.

The power of reading for pleasure means that, as parents and educators, we need to put aside our own thoughts on what children should be reading. Kids enjoy reading the most when they can escape into a book with no expectations, when they don't have to worry about analysing themes or other literary devices a parent or teacher may want them to learn from the book.

To get a better understanding of what your own child or your students enjoy about free-choice reading, it is helpful to ask some of the following questions. Do keep in mind that this will just be a snapshot of their reading at this particular point in time.

- What has been your favourite book recently?
- What do you think is the purpose of reading? Why do you think we need to read?
- If you could read any type of book at all what would you choose to read?
- Have you had times when you have read like a demon? Explain in your own words.
- Have you had times when you've read very little? Explain in your own words.
- What book was your favourite when you were really little?
- Have you ever become obsessed by a particular series? What do you think you liked most about this series?
- How do you choose books to read?
- How do you share what you read with your friends and what do you tell them about it?
- Do you re-read favourite books?

It may seem odd to move from a discussion on free-choice reading to a section on reading widely. However, I believe the two ideas can sit side by side and even play nicely without whacking each other over the head, trying to prove who is more important.

I like to compare a balanced literary diet to a balanced food diet and ask children what might happen if they decided to eat only pineapple for the rest of their life. As much as they may love pineapple, it wouldn't be healthy because we need to eat a range of foods from the various food groups to grow healthy and strong. And so it is with reading. We might *think* we will enjoy living on a diet of adventure novels, but eventually our brain will cry out for something more, something different. Like our body, our brain needs variety in order to grow.

Encouraging young people to read widely and enjoy a balanced literary diet can add immeasurably to their enjoyment of recreational reading. Think about your own reading tastes. Sometimes you may yearn for dark, intense crime and other times you want nothing more than a light, fluffy romance. Being made aware of a genre you didn't even know existed can open reading doorways and lead to all manner of literary adventures. Below I've outlined a range of book genres and explored the benefits young readers may gain by engaging with them.

HUMOUR

I was sitting next to a group of mothers at a coffee shop and I heard them bemoaning their children's choice of reading material: 'If I have to listen to one more ridiculous Treehouse story I am going to—' You get the idea. I kept my eyes on the book I was reading and my mouth full of espresso, but in my mind I turned around and said, 'You are so lucky you have children who love reading. This joy they are experiencing thanks to Andy Griffiths and Terry Denton will stand them in good stead as readers. Plus they *rock*.'

Too often adults dismiss humorous books as not as worthy as 'highbrow' literary choices, and I admit I have been guilty of this. Engaging young people, particularly reluctant readers, with books they adore is how we create readers. Writers like Andy Griffiths,

David Walliams, Terry Denton, Miranda Hart, Cath Cassidy, Roald Dahl, Michael Gerard Bauer, R. A. Spratt, and Matt Stanton have all used their wit and sense of humour to entertain, heal with laughter, educate and instil a love of reading in young people.

Why encourage the reading of humour

- Humour engages children (particularly reluctant readers) as they are naturally playful and generally laugh far more than adults. Humorous literature harnesses the exuberance and wonder of youth with words and ideas.
- Young people interact and foster friendships through humorous literature as they enjoy sharing the laughs with their peers.
- Humorous books reflect reality, which is a mixture of sad and funny, joy and pain, highs and lows.
- Far from being an 'easy option', humorous literature encourages critical reading as young people learn to read between the lines and develop an awareness of subtlety and sarcasm, right and wrong.

For each genre I've included a list of recommended books suitable for the eight- to fourteen-year-old age group. These lists are by no means prescriptive and are merely springboards for you to find your own favourites. Please check the appropriateness of a book for each individual reader.

Misery Guts series by Morris Gleitzman (Pan Macmillan Australia)

The Bad Guys series by Aaron Blabey (Scholastic Australia)

Con-Nerd series and others by Oliver Phommavanh (Penguin Books Australia)

Tom Weekly series by Tristan Bancks and Gus Gordon (Random House Australia Children's)

Dog Man series by Dav Pilkey (Scholastic US)

Toad Rage series by Morris Gleitzman (Penguin Books)

Don't Call Me Ishmael by Michael Gerard Bauer (HarperCollins Publishers Inc., 2007) (upper end of age group)

The Bugalugs Bum Thief by Tim Winton, illustrated by Stephen Michael King (Penguin Books, 2003)

The Stinky Street Stories series by Alex Ratt, illustrated by Jules Faber (Pan Macmillan Australia)

Mr Bambuckle's Remarkables series by Tim Harris, illustrated by James Hart (Random House Australia)

WeirDo series by Anh Do, illustrated by Jules Faber (Scholastic Australia)

Samurai Vs Ninja series by Nick Falk and Tony Flowers (Random House Australia)

Captain Jimmy Cook Discovers by Kate and Jol Temple, illustrated by Jon Foye (Allen & Unwin, 2017)

Eric Vale series by Michael Gerard Bauer, illustrated by Joe Bauer (Scholastic Australia)

Gastronauts by James Foley (Fremantle Press, 2018)

A Roman Garstang Adventure series by Mark Lowery (Templar Publishing)

Beatrice Zinker Upside Down Thinker series by Shelley Johannes (Hachette Australia)

The Shrinking of Treehorn by Florence Parry Heide, illustrated by Edward Gorey (Holiday House Inc, 1992)

Penny Pollard series by Robin Klein and Ann James (Hachette Australia)

Ramona series by Beverly Cleary, illustrated by Jacqueline Rogers (HarperCollins Publishers Inc.)

MYSTERY

I was never into mystery stories as a child and it wasn't until my mid-twenties when my mother introduced me to Agatha Christie's most popular sleuth, Hercule Poirot, and Donna Leon's Commissario Guido Brunetti that I became an avid reader of mystery. There is something mildly addictive about figuring out what will happen next and putting all the pieces of a puzzle together. For many young readers, mysteries contain the excitement of a life far removed from their own suburban existence. Young protagonists who lead investigations, collect and study the evidence, and solve mysteries are inspiring to the would-be detectives of tomorrow or simply those who have a curious mind and sense of adventure.

Not only are they fun and usually fast-paced page turners, but mystery novels helps young readers to read critically, consider cause and effect, logical deduction, and how vital information and facts may be collected.

I've asked bestselling author R. A. Spratt to share the elements she includes in her Friday Barnes, Nanny Piggins and Pesky Kids series to create stories with tension and intrigue.

R. A. Spratt

I don't know how I create tension and intrigue to hook young readers in. I really have no idea what I'm doing and I haven't done for twenty years now. I believe that storytelling is a magical art and you can't explain magic.

I'm not speaking figuratively. I literally mean magical. My ideas start out as nothing more than electrical energy passing between the neurons in my brain. This electricity conjures up images, voices and motivations in my mind which I blend together in a web of ideas. I take the twenty-six squiggles that are the letters in the Romanised alphabet and transcribe them into a computer. This is printed up and sold to thousands of children and libraries. Then the squiggles are decoded into the mind of the reader. Between my neurons and their neurons an entire world is created full of characters we care for much more than we do the living breathing characters we live alongside in real life. A reader's heart will race, they'll laugh, they'll shed a tear as they go on a journey with my characters. To me this is pure magic, or at the very least a miracle of neuroscience and biochemistry.

As to intrigue and tension – I'm not sure about tension so I'll start with intrigue. I once heard a radio interview with an acclaimed novelist (I can't remember who) and she said that from reading Dickens she had learned that the trick to storytelling was figuring out the story you wanted to tell and then telling it very slowly (I think she said this in a much cleverer way, but I heard this interview decades ago so I can't remember her exact words).

I always think of storytelling as laying a trail of breadcrumbs to lead someone along a path. Which is actually a terrible misuse of an analogy because Hansel and Gretel laid breadcrumbs to lead themselves back, not to lead someone else forward ... in any case, storytelling is entirely linear. The line can go in circles and double back but you write out the ideas one sentence after another, always moving forward (except if you write pick-a-path books, which might explain why those books are emotionally unsatisfying). To make a story intriguing the trick is to not lay down an entire loaf of bread at the beginning of the path. If you put down a whole loaf the birds eat the bread until they are full and then they fly away. You've got to lay out one crumb at a time if you want the bird to follow you.

To write a mystery novel you, as the author know, the whole plot in your head but you've got to deal this information out one piece at a time. To keep the story moving forward, every sentence you write should forward the plot or develop character or both. But in mystery, it is good to deal out misinformation as well. It makes the characters more interesting and it gives the reader more to think about.

Tension comes from the readers caring about the characters or the resolution of the plot. They usually care more about the characters so if you can make the problem of the plot intertwine with the problems of your characters, you double down on tension.

Two Wolves by Tristan Bancks (Random House Australia, 2014)
Missing by Sue Whiting (Walker Books Australia, 2018)
10 Rules for Detectives by Kierin Meehan (Penguin eBooks, 2008)
Del-Del by Victor Kelleher (Random House Australia Children's, 2000)
Withering-by-Sea by Judith Rossell (ABC Books, 2014)
Crow Country by Kate Constable (Allen & Unwin, 2011)
Henry Hoey Hobson by Christine Bongers (Random House Australia, 2016)
Someone Like Me by Elaine Forrestal (Penguin Books Australia, 1997)
Mosquito Advertising: The Parfizz Pitch by Kate Hunter (University of Queensland Press, 2010)
The London Eye Mystery by Siobhan Dowd (Penguin Books, 2016)
Friday Barnes series by R. A. Spratt (Random House Australia)
Kat Wolfe Investigates by Lauren St John (Pan Macmillan, 2018)
Every series by Ellie Marney (Allen & Unwin) (older readers)
Found by Fleur Ferris (Penguin Books Australia, 2018) (older readers)
Catching Teller Crow by Ambelin Kwaymullina & Ezekiel Kwaymullina (Allen & Unwin, 2018) (older readers)

HISTORICAL FICTION

A good historical novel leads the reader through adventures of the past, bringing real historical events to life. I personally have learnt more about Australian history through reading Jackie French's novels, than I did in all my years of history lessons at school. Learning about the past helps us to understand the world today and perhaps even prepare for the future by recognising mistakes which must not be repeated. Historical fiction personalises accounts of past atrocities, which helps us to develop greater empathy than if we were to read a strictly factual account of the same historical event.

Historical fiction books are set in vastly different eras, from ancient Egypt and medieval Italy to colonial Australia, so young readers may need help understanding the specific context. They should also be encouraged to read a few chapters before deciding to abandon a book. It can take longer than usual for a reader to find their groove in a historical fiction book, but the effort required is worth it when you see your child fall through the cracks of history and into a fabulous tale.

The Blue Cat by Ursula Dubosarsky (Allen & Unwin, 2017)

The Ratcatcher's Daughter by Pamela Rushby (HarperCollins Publishers, 2014)

The River Charm (and others in series) by Belinda Murrell (Penguin Books Australia, 2013)

The Silver Donkey by Sonya Hartnett (Penguin Books Australia, 2007)

The Children of the King by Sonya Hartnett (Scholastic Australia, 2014)

Hitler's Daughter by Jackie French (Harper Collins Publishers, 1999)

Macbeth and Son by Jackie French (Harper Collins, 2006)

Yong by Janeen Brian (Walker Books Australia, 2016)

The War that Saved My Life by Kimberly Brubaker Bradley (Text Publishing, 2016)

A Long Walk to Water by Linda Sue Park (University of Queensland Press, 2011)

When My Name Was Keoko by Linda Sue Park (University of Queensland Press, 2013)

Daughter of the Regiment by Jackie French (Angus & Robertson, 1998)

The Burnt Stick by Anthony Hill, illustrated by Mark Sofilas (Penguin Books Australia, 1996)

A Rose for the Anzac Boys by Jackie French (HarperCollins Publishers, 2008)

That Boy, Jack by Janeen Brian (Walker Books Australia, 2013)

Lighthouse Girl by Dianne Wolfer, illustrated by Brian Simmonds (Fremantle Press, 2009)

Light Horse Boy by Dianne Wolfer, illustrated by Brian Simmonds (Fremantle Press, 2013)

In the Lamplight by Dianne Wolfer, illustrated by Brian Simmonds (Fremantle Press, 2018)

Taj and the Great Camel Trek by Rosanne Hawke (University of Queensland Press, 2011)

REALISTIC FICTION

Contemporary realistic fiction are stories that are believable and set in the modern world. These works of fiction explore plausible conflicts and contain characters who seem real and identifiable. What puts the 'real' in realistic fiction are the themes – they touch on all that is wonderful and confronting about being a human today. Common contemporary themes explore family situations, peer relationships, growth and maturity and cultural differences.

These stories have so much to offer. They help children address their own physical, social and emotional changes, and provide role models who are facing tough situations. They can also help children discover that their problems and desires are not unique – that they are not alone in experiencing certain feelings and situations.

On the other hand, realistic fiction may also provide a gateway for kids to experience someone else's 'real' life – the life of another young person, perhaps on the other side of the world. They can see that societies are not all the same and that different communities hold diverse values and customs. In effect, realistic fiction can help children to develop an awareness of how there are many different perspectives in this world whilst, at the same time, fostering an appreciation for all that we have in common.

Belinda Murrell is the author of many award-winning novels for children and teens and writes over a large range of genres from fantasy to historical fiction and realistic fiction. Her most recent series, Pippa's Island, is a fine example of realistic fiction writing and she has shared her thoughts on the genre here.

Belinda Murrell

I grew up in a book-mad family and as well as devouring piles of books every week I adored writing my own stories. When I had my three children, I began writing stories for them, very much inspired by what my kids loved to read. And although my first stories – both as a child and as an author – were full of magic and adventure, such as the Sun Sword trilogy and historical time-slip novels and mysteries, my most recent stories have been about friends, families and animal adventures.

My latest series is called Pippa's Island and my aim was to write sparkling books set in a realistic world about a fun-loving girl and her friends. I wanted to celebrate the joyful, inspiring, funny, kind, creative, caring, sassy girls I know.

On one level the stories are about everyday life at school, hanging out on weekends, embarrassing yourself in dance class, dealing with stage fright at the school talent quest or going away on your first school camp. The series also deals with issues such as making friends, the importance of community, finding courage, standing up for what's right and coping with change.

One of my key aims was to create quirky characters who were inspiring role models for readers. The main characters are realistic in their emotions – sometimes cranky, jealous, prickly or anxious, but also kind, brave and compassionate. The girls all have their own aspirations – whether it is to become a vet, an artist or an engineer, to save wildlife or travel the world. Likewise, the older women in their lives have interesting careers such as a stockbroker, fashion designer, musician, marine biologist and graphic designer.

Stories about real life are like a mirror, helping children to understand how to navigate human relationships and solve everyday problems of friendship, families, sibling rivalry, school, sport and emotions.

On the other hand, realistic books can also provide a window into the lives of others, giving children the opportunity to walk around in someone else's shoes. To understand how different people might think and feel. For this reason, I ensure my books portray diverse and imperfect families, and characters from different social and cultural backgrounds.

Research has shown that reading fiction helps children to build emotional intelligence and to develop empathy for other people by exploring others' thoughts, perspectives and experiences. As well as building compassion for others, reading realistic books helps them to realise that their own personal problems and fears are not unique. They are not alone in the world.

Realistic fiction helps young readers realise that life is a constant rollercoaster of ups and downs, and not always easy. But while there are disappointments and difficulties along the way, there is always joy and hope, a theme celebrated in all my books.

Just a Dog by Michael Gerard Bauer (Scholastic Australia, 2010)
Figgy series by Tamsin Janu (Scholastic Australia)
The Grand Genius Summer of Henry Hoobler by Lisa Shanahan (Allen & Unwin, 2017)
Mrs Whitlam by Bruce Pascoe (Magabala Books, 2016)
Sea Horse by Bruce Pascoe (Magabala Books, 2015)
The Elephant by Peter Carnavas (University of Queensland Press, 2017)
The Secret Science of Magic by Melissa Keil (Hardie Grant Egmont, 2017) (older readers)
Kingdom of Silk series by Glenda Millard (HarperCollins/ABC Books)

Wonder by R. J. Palacio (Random House Children's Publishers UK, 2014)

Everything I've Never Said by Samantha Wheeler (University of Queensland Press, 2018)

Two Hands Together by Diana Kidd (Penguin Books Australia, 2000)

Boss of the Pool by Robin Klein (Scholastic Australia, 2001)

Lockie Leonard, Legend by Tim Winton (Penguin Books Australia, 2013)

A Bridge to Wiseman's Cove by James Moloney (University of Queensland Press, 2007) (older readers)

My Big Birkett by Lisa Shanahan (Allen & Unwin, 2006)

The Secrets We Keep by Nova Weetman (University of Queensland Press, 2016)

My Girragundji by Meme McDonald and Boori Pryor (Allen & Unwin, 2018)

Matty Forever by Elizabeth Fensham (University of Queensland Press, 2009)

Unrequited by Emma Grey (HarperCollins Publishers, 2017) (older readers)

Black Cockatoo by Carl Merrison and Hakea Hustler (Magabala Books, 2018)

FANTASY

It's impossible to overstate the powerful and positive effect Harry Potter had on children's publishing, particularly the fantasy genre. Its popularity allowed other authors to venture down their own magical paths and create young worthy heroes who battle evil, usually with the support of a mentor and a collection of friends. The beauty of fantasy lies with its capacity for variation and unexpected wonder. Some authors incorporate magical elements into our ordinary existence, others place their characters (and their readers) into a fantastical realm.

Just as adults like to escape from the monotony of real life, children also need to indulge in pure escapism. Fantasy can be that space. Imagining being friends with a witch, hunting down demon robot dogs, or protecting innocent unicorns. Reading fantasy and imagining the worlds within also help fire up creative processes. They can also enhance critical thinking skills, particularly in books where the depicted political and socioeconomic systems are complex and mirror our own. Young people can advance their knowledge of government and explore other political and social issues. So fantasy is not just about readers escaping the real world, but gaining a more sophisticated understanding of it and hopefully becoming mature and thoughtful citizens of the world.

The Garden of Empress Cassia by Gabrielle Wang (Penguin Books Australia, 2002)

The Pearl of Tiger Bay by Gabrielle Wang (Penguin Books Australia, 2004)

Victor's Quest by Pamela Freeman (Walker Books Australia, 2008)

Bartlett and the Ice Voyage by Odo Hirsch (Allen & Unwin, 1998)

Refuge by Jackie French (HarperCollins Publishers, 2013)

Ranger's Apprentice series by John Flanagan (Random House)

Dragonkeeper series by Carole Wilkinson (Black Dog Books)

The Four Seasons of Lucy McKenzie by Kirsty Murray (Allen & Unwin, 2013)

Ophelia and the Marvellous Boy by Karen Foxlee (Hot Key Books, 2017)

The Extremely Inconvenient Adventures of Bronte Mettlestone by Jaclyn Moriarty (Allen & Unwin, 2017)

The Mapmaker Chronicles series and The Ateban Cipher series by A. L. Tait (Hachette)

The Obernewtyn series, The Legend of Little Fur series and The Kingdom of the Lost series by Isobelle Carmody

The Song of the Lioness series and The Protector of the Small series by Tamora Pierce

Rowan of Rin series by Emily Rodda (Scholastic Australia)

The Keys to the Kingdom series by Garth Nix (Allen & Unwin)

Deltora Quest series by Emily Rodda (Scholastic Australia)

SCIENCE FICTION

Science fiction (sci-fi) has traditionally been associated with futuristic space novels where alien life and other planets featured heavily. Technology has also been a major component of this genre. But sci-fi actually incorporates many different sub-categories and, over the past two decades, authors have been mashing these up to create new and original genres. For example, writers have merged history with technology to create steampunk or placed post-apocalypse survivors into dictatorial environments to make dystopian sci-fi. The prevalence of innovation within the genre means it remains highly sought-after for young readers. Science fiction can be defined by its setting and technological content, but within these boundaries there is so much scope to explore – an artificial intelligent detective turns sci-fi into a crime thriller, a boy from one planet falling in love with a girl from an opposing species produces a *Romeo and Juliet* equivalent, and an intergalactic broadcast of celebrities fighting on a reality TV program makes a biting satire on fame. And for younger readers, authors can still promote messages of kindness, friendship and acceptance through a speculative lens. Humorous alien-life stories are very popular, but even when they are less so, there will always be the curious reader who gazes out beyond the air pollution to imagine what's up there among the stars.

Blossom by Tamsin Janu (Scholastic Australia, 2017)
The Red Wind by Isobelle Carmody (Penguin Books Australia, 2011)
Space Demons by Gillian Rubinstein (Scholastic, 1986)
Skymaze by Gillian Rubinstein (Omnibus/Puffin, 1989)
Deucalion by Brian Caswell (University of Queensland Press, 1995)
The Lake at the End of the World by Caroline Macdonald (Penguin Books Australia, 1995)
Grimsdon by Deborah Abela (Random House Australia, 2014)
Galactic Adventures: First Kids in Space by Tristan Bancks (University of Queensland Press, 2011)
A Small Free Kiss in the Dark by Glenda Millard (Allen & Unwin, 2009) (older readers)
The Phoenix Files series by Chris Morphew (Hardie Grant Egmont) (older readers)
In the Dark Spaces by Cally Black (Hardie Grant Egmont, 2017) (older readers)
The Lunar Chronicles series by Marissa Meyer (Penguin) (older readers)
Carve the Mark by Veronica Roth (for older readers) (HarperCollins, 2016)
What Goes Up by Katie Kennedy (Bloomsbury, 2018) (older readers)

DYSTOPIAN FICTION

Dystopian novels have existed as long as writers have questioned political systems and the extent to which they control our lives. Just as Jules Verne, H. G. Wells, and Jonathan Swift challenged readers of their time with their ideologies, so too did George Orwell and Aldous Huxley, Lois Lowry and Margaret Atwood. But it was really Suzanne Collins's Hunger Games series that made the genre once again on trend in children's and YA literature.

The opposite of utopia, dystopia is the idea that society will be controlled by beings in power and people will be devoid of freewill. It is an idea that fascinates us all, even young people, and perhaps especially today when our world seems to be more divided than ever. Placing protagonists into an uncertain future is another way for readers to ponder the calamities of their own time. Allowing young people to ask serious questions about how they want the world to develop encourages problem-solving, a strong desire for compassion and critical thinking skills.

These books are long lasting and remain relevant over time. Orwell's doublespeak seems to be around us everywhere and unless we open a dialogue with our children about some of the troubling things happening, we are perhaps doomed to repeat the mistakes of the past.

A sub-genre within the dystopian category is the post-apocalyptic novel, which sees the breakdown of society. Instead of a controlling regime, ordered and secretive, we have total chaos and devastation. Sometimes it's due to natural weather events or a deadly pandemic virus or overloaded computer systems causing technological annihilation. In these novels children are exposed to survival efforts that can be vicious and scary, or collaborative and positive, as communities band together to benefit all. Often the latter are presented as adventure stories with the emphasis less on social commentary and more on the action so they are gripping and engaging.

How to Bee by Bren MacDibble (Allen & Unwin, 2017)

A Single Stone by Meg McKinlay (Walker Books Australia, 2015)

Mechanica (2016) and *Aquatica* (2017) by Lance Balchin (The Five Mile Press)

Hive by A. J. Betts (Pan Macmillan, 2018) (older readers)

The Giver by Lois Lowry (Houghton Mifflin, 1993) (older readers)

Divergent series by Veronica Roth (Harper Collins) (older readers)

Uglies series by Scott Westerfeld (Simon & Schuster) (older readers)

The Tribe series by Ambelin Kwaymullina (Penguin Random House) (older readers)

The Maze Runner series by James Dashner (Delacorte Press, 2009)

When the Lights Go Out by Lili Wilkinson (Allen & Unwin, 2018) (older readers)

The Road to Winter (plus sequels) by Mark Smith (Text Publishing, 2016) (older readers)

The Pandora Jones series by Barry Jonsberg (Allen & Unwin) (older readers)

The Sky So Heavy by Claire Zorn (University of Queensland Press, 2013) (older readers)

MYTHS, LEGENDS AND FAIRYTALES

Though separate genres, in a sense, myths, legends and fairytales fall under the umbrella term 'traditional tales'. They come in and out of favour and well-meaning censors can be critical of messages sent to, say, young girls who may feel they need saving by a Prince Charming. But I think they offer us escape from reality and a framework to consider our place in world and ourselves as humans. Sophie Masson is a multiple award-winning French-Australian author of over 50 books, many of which are based on myths, legends and fairytales. There is simply no other person more qualified to comment on traditional tales and, as she said to me recently, 'they are absolutely essential for the development of children's reading, ideas and imagination'.

....

Sophie Masson

As a child I adored the myths of Greek and Celtic heroes, Norse gods, Chinese star-crossed lovers; the legends of King Arthur and Robin Hood; the fairytales of Perrault and Grimm and Hans Christian Andersen. I returned again and again to my favourites and was drawn to novels that used elements from these stories, such as Nicholas Stuart Gray's superb *The Stone Cage*, which is a glorious riff on the fairytale of Rapunzel. (Why it is out of print beats me, especially as it has been cited as a huge influence by many well-known fantasy writers, including Neil Gaiman.) Without even being aware of it, through all this reading, I was absorbing all kinds of things that would stand me in good stead later as a writer. Myths, legends and fairytales are different genres yet they form part of a great human inheritance which is very often anonymous, at least in its sources, and yet very distinctively individual. They offer questions and potential, not answers and certainties; despite the censors' claims, they are not prescriptive, even though they can certainly seem arbitrary. And for a writer they offer multiple creative interpretations and possibilities: for instance, going back to Cinderella, I never saw it as girl-saved-by-Prince-Charming (who in fact, in the fairytale, is a cipher, and the really important characters are all female, both the good and the bad). Here, instead, for me, is a story of a neglected, abused child, who, through the kindness of a stranger, is finally given an opportunity to escape into a different, happier life. That is certainly how I interpreted it in my novel *Moonlight and Ashes*.

Introducing these stories to children is easy; there are multiple retellings of the great myths, legends and fairytales around, aimed at different ages and reading levels, from lavishly illustrated picture books to graphic novels to compilations such as Roger Lancelyn Green's classic *Tales of the Greek*

Heroes. Countless well-known contemporary authors have tackled retellings, including Ursula Dubosarsky (*Two Tales of Twins from Ancient Greece and Rome*), John Heffernan (*Two Tales of Brothers from Ancient Mesopotamia*) and Anthony Horowitz (*The Kingfisher Book of Myths and Legends*). These tales, drawn from around the world, with their adventures, magic and fantastical creatures, are also really well-suited to lively storytelling sessions. Later, young readers can be introduced to fantastic novels that use these traditional tales as inspiration: for instance, Rick Riordan's Percy Jackson series, *Ella Enchanted* by Gail Carson Levine, *I Was a Rat!* by Philip Pullman, T. H. White's *The Once and Future King*, Lloyd Alexander's *The Chronicles of Prydain* and many others too numerous to mention. Young adult readers are also well served with lots of great novels out there based on myth, legend and fairytale. And you can keep reading in these genres well into adulthood – in fact, all of your life. They will never get stale – their very magic and wonder have kept them alive for thousands of years and I think they are every child's inheritance.

The Great Deeds of Superheroes by Maurice Saxby, illustrated by Robert Ingpen (Millennium, 1989)

The Voyage of the Poppykettle by Robert Ingpen (Rigby, 1980)

Two Trickster Tales from Russia retold by Sophie Masson, illustrated by David Allan (Christmas Press, 2013)

Two Selkie Stories from Scotland retold by Kate Forsyth, illustrated by Fiona McDonald (Christmas Press, 2014)

Two Tales of Twins from Ancient Greece and Rome retold by Ursula Dubosarsky, illustrated by David Allan (Christmas Press, 2014)

Two Tengu Tales from Japan retold by Duncan Ball, illustrated by David Allan (Christmas Press, 2015)

Norse Myths: Tales of Odin, Thor and Loki by Kevin Cressley-Holland, illustrated by Jeffrey Alan Love (Walker Studio, 2017)

THE CLASSICS

The debate about whether or not the 'classics' are still relevant for young readers is one that pops up repeatedly. It is a debate that often emerges in response to the changing state and national school curriculums, but also because so much quality and 'edgy' contemporary literature is available now. It is a constant challenge to find a balance between material that young people will immediately engage with and respond to and introducing them to something that might taste a bit strange at first bite but will ultimately be quite satisfying. Seeing readers 'get' Shakespeare or Austen or Orwell is a magical moment. The 'classics' are great stories. They are classics because they are the milestones of literary tradition, originally breaking away from established ideas or challenging the status quo of the time. They are classics because they are still the best at what they 'do' and are part of a literary history that influences the work of contemporary writers. Having some knowledge or understanding of the classics makes the references in contemporary fiction have a deeper meaning and engagement.

At least once in a student's secondary schooling they will be asked to read a modern classic - maybe *Lord of the Flies*, *To Kill a Mockingbird* or *The Outsiders*. Usually these books contain a different style of writing, an increasingly disappearing vocabulary and a perspective that may be verging on political incorrectness. Exposing children to some of these texts outside the classroom means they will have some knowledge when they are confronted with them on school reading lists.

Reading modern classics is a satisfying way to access history. Take *The Catcher in the Rye* (J. D. Salinger) as an example. It has captured the first glimpse of the concept of the adolescent. Before the creation of the character Holden Caulfield, we were children and then we were adults. The teenage years in a person's life were pretty much ignored. This novel also coincided with the beginnings of an economic boom, the start of popular culture, increased leisure time, greater equality for women and the birth of rock 'n' roll. To bring these days alive so vividly to young people and ask them to reflect on what has changed and what hasn't is a sure way to engage them in their own history and culture. Australian modern classics from *Picnic at Hanging Rock* to *The Fringe Dwellers* depict our past, unique landscape and cultural identity and capture how important it is to tell our own stories. Just a few examples of modern classics are listed below.

Playing Beatie Bow by Ruth Park (Penguin Books Australia, 1982)
My Sister Sif by Ruth Park (University of Queensland Press, 2009)
The Best-Kept Secret by Emily Rodda (HarperCollins, 2017)
The Nargun and the Stars by Patricia Wrightson (University of Queensland Press, 2008)
Storm Boy by Colin Thiele (Rigby, 1963)
The Listmaker by Robin Klein (Penguin Books Australia, 2016)
Swashbuckler by James Moloney (University of Queensland Press, 1995)
45+47 Stella Street and Everything That Happened by Elizabeth Honey (Allen & Unwin, 2000)
Looking for Alibrandi by Melina Marchetta (Penguin Books Australia, 1992)
Thunderwith by Libby Hathorn (Hachette Australia, 1999)
Little Brother by Allan Baillie (Penguin Books Australia, 2004)
Hating Alison Ashley by Robin Klein (Penguin Books Australia, 1985)
Midnite by Randolph Stow (Penguin Books Australia, 2004)

NON-FICTION

There are children who love nothing more than reading every non-fiction book in the library. These children crack me up with their encyclopaedic knowledge of sharks, deserts, the body or whatever their current obsession is, and I really enjoy having a natter to them. Equally, there are many children who struggle with non-fiction texts. They seem much happier following a narrative and always resist borrowing the non-fiction books I try to slide their way. If you have a reader who is resistant to non-fiction books, I often start with cooking or craft books as these have a clear purpose and a positive outcome such as a delicious meal or cute sock puppet. Or I'll suggest doing some gardening and then use non-fiction books to find out the information we need. Another trick is to have a peer recommend a non-fiction book they have really enjoyed, often on a topic loved by all such as pets or Australian mammals.

Non-fiction books form a part of a balanced reading diet and are incredibly useful in exposing children to a wide range of genres and text types. Modern non-fiction books rely heavily on good design with eye-catching graphics and varied typography and layout, which are intended to make complex concepts more easily accessible and interesting. These design features encourage non-linear reading and mimic the interactive nature of browsing online. Readers can dip in and out of non-fiction books, making them perfect for reading in small chunks. They also don't require a sustained level of attention so wriggly or reluctant readers are often kept engaged.

Non-fiction books expand our knowledge in a diverse range of subjects and help build up a solid foundation of general knowledge in younger readers. In the various areas of interest and study, not only is knowledge expanded but vocabulary is too. We read non-fiction to learn how to navigate information effectively - in both print and digital form. The best non-fiction books contain a contents page, index and glossary, to help children find areas of interest quickly and to develop an understanding of how information is organised in headings or subject areas. Non-fiction books expose children to a huge variety of text types and visual aids like diagrams, graphs, captions, lists, headings, subheadings and labels.

Ned Kelly's The Jerilderie Letter edited by Carole Wilkinson, illustrated by Dean Jones (Black Dog Books, 2007)

Spellbound: Making Pictures with the ABC by Maree Coote (Melbournestyle Books, 2015)

Maralinga's Long Shadow by Christobel Mattingley (Allen & Unwin, 2016)

The Word Spy by Ursula Dubosarsky, illustrated by Tohby Riddle (Penguin Books Australia, 2011)

The Greatest Gatsby by Tohby Riddle (Penguin Books Australia, 2015)

The Girl from the Great Sandy Desert by Jukuna Mona Chuguna and Pat Lowe, illustrated by Mervyn Street (Magabala Books, 2015)

Wicked Warriors & Evil Emperors: The True Story for the Fight for Ancient China (2017), *Devils and Rebels* (2017) and *The Upside Down History of Down Under* (2018) by Alison Lloyd, illustrated by Terry Denton (Penguin Books Australia)

Maralinga, The Anangu Story by Yalata and Oak Valley Communities with Christobel Mattingley (Allen & Unwin, 2012)

Phasmid: Saving the Lord Howe Island Stick Insect by Rohan Cleave and Coral Tulloch (CSIRO Publishing, 2015)

Limelight by Solli Raphael (Puffin, 2018)

Growing up Aboriginal in Australia edited by Anita Heiss (Black Inc Books, 2018) (older readers)

BIOGRAPHIES AND AUTOBIOGRAPHIES

For young readers who choose to read non-fiction almost exclusively, biographies and autobiographies can be a soft introduction to the power of story while still sticking with facts (with any luck!). Reading biographical works introduces young readers to iconic personalities. Many biographical works are available in 'younger reader' formats, and compendiums of famous or inspiring individuals are really popular too.

It is fascinating to take a look at someone's life and gain a better understanding of the ideas and motivations that helped them to succeed or overcome adversity. The stories can be truly awe-inspiring. Which leads me to my next point - I am a big fan of using books to help young people to see life through a different lens. My hope for today's children is that they never have to experience traumas such as war or poverty, but by reading about others who have overcome enormous hurdles they develop empathy, social responsibility and a sense of gratitude.

History often comes alive for children when they read personal accounts and real-life stories. Biographical works are a great way for children to see the chronology and significance of historical events, including how the past impacts the present. Current world events may also start to make more sense when viewed from a historical perspective.

Ugly by Robert Hoge (Hachette Australia, 2015)

Mao's Last Dancer by Li Cunxin (younger readers' edition) (Penguin, 2006)

On Two Feet and Wings by Abbas Kazerooni (Allen & Unwin, 2012)

Chinese Cinderella by Adeline Yen Mah (Penguin, 1999)

El Deafo by Cece Bell (Abrams, 2014) (also graphic novel)

Finding Nevo by Nevo Zisin (Black Dog Books, 2017) (older readers)

Boy by Roald Dahl (Penguin, 1984)

Jandamarra by Mark Greenwood, illustrated by Terry Denton (Allen & Unwin, 2013)

Kimberley Warrior: The Story of Jandamarra by John Nicholson (Allen & Unwin, 2001)

Say Hello by Carly Findlay (HarperCollins, 2019) (older readers)

Unmasked – YA edition by Turia Pitt (Penguin Books Australia, 2018) (older readers)

The Happiest Refugee by Anh Do (Allen & Unwin, 2010) (older readers)

PLAYS AND FILM SCRIPTS

We all know *the* rule. The rule of all rules. You should never, *ever* see a movie before you have read the book. It is a rule many of us live and die by. Yet for some strange reason we all seem to think that you shouldn't *read* a play or film script; you should go see the play or film. Just as you would miss out by not reading that book before heading to the cinema, there is a lot to be lost by not considering plays and scripts as a form of literature.

The white space between the dialogue and stage directions is simply filled with potential. Readers are invited to work hard to imagine what these moments might look and sound like. Scripts inspire us to use our mind's eye and visualise the characters' world as if it were appearing before us, almost hologram-like. We are not given lengthy descriptions and internal monologues with which to make sense of what is happening, but, instead, must use inference and deduction – two incredibly important skills required to be a strong reader.

Plays, given that they are essentially transcriptions of speech, often focus on the dynamics and relationships between characters – the drama, conflict, actions, reactions and resolutions. There is rarely a narrator and limited authorial intrusion so readers can get up close and personal and really see how meaning is made without lengthy exposition. They can become intimate with the text by observing what the characters say and do.

Reading plays and scripts also exposes young people to language that is often poetic and rhythmic. The playwright and scriptwriter must be economical in the way they craft their story and consider how their words will sound spoken aloud on stage. By reading plays and scripts younger readers gain a greater appreciation of the power of deliberate language choices, and the fun that can be had with words.

Of course we also want to introduce our children to the joy and wonder of seeing live theatre or beautifully produced films, but there is something to be said for reading plays and scripts and encouraging our young readers to perform those words in their own head, in their own voices, before seeing them interpreted by another on the stage or screen.

Hating Alison Ashley: The Play by Richard Tulloch (based on the novel by Robin Klein) (Penguin Books Australia, 1988)

Stage Fright: Four Wacky Plays by Richard Tulloch (Puffin Books, 1996)

Two Weeks with the Queen: The Play adapted by Mary Morris (based on the novel by Morris Gleitzman) (Currency Press, 2011)

Jasper Jones adapted by Kate Mulvany (based on the novel by Craig Silvey) (Currency Press, 2017)

Boy Overboard: The Play adapted by Patricia Cornelius (based on the novel by Morris Gleitzman) (Currency Press, 2007)

SHORT STORIES

The short story is an underrated form. It is the one that young people are most often asked to write, and yet, according to NAPLAN data, often the one in which they do most poorly. To be able to create a story, complete yet concise and satisfying, is a highly demanding exercise. Writers such as Dahl and Bradbury perfected this art with much practise and talent. Children are very lucky that some of the best authors including David Malouf, Tim Winton, and Peter Carey started out in short story writing and have many offerings for them to study.

Short stories are also valuable for young people who struggle to get through a novel. It allows them to achieve a sense of completion without too much frustration or fear of failure. Short stories also come in a range of genres, so it's easy to find something that a child might like - whether it be humour, adventure, or mystery. By understanding the conventions of the format, young people will be more confident and capable with their own narrative writing.

Funny Stories and Other Funny Stories by Morris Gleitzman (Penguin Books Australia, 2018)

The Book of Horses and Unicorns by Jackie French (HarperCollins, 2014)

Total Quack Up edited by Sally Rippin and Adrian Beck, illustrated by James Foley (Penguin Books Australia, 2018)

My Life and Other Stuff I Made Up by Tristan Bancks (Random House Australia, 2014)

The Hush Treasure Book by Hush Foundation (Allen & Unwin, 2015)

Rich and Rare edited by Paul Collins (Ford Street Publishing, 2015)

Give Peas a Chance by Morris Gleitzman (Penguin Books Australia, 2007)

Begin, End, Begin: A #LoveOzYA Anthology edited by Danielle Binks (HarperCollins, 2018) (older readers)

Bush and Beyond by Tjalaminu Mia, Jessica Lister, Jaylon Tucker and Cheryl Kickett-Tucker (Freemantle Press, 2018)

Unreal! The Ultimate Collection by Paul Jennings (Penguin Books Australia, 2015)

Meet Me at the Intersection edited by Rebecca Lim and Ambelin Kwaymullina (Freemantle Press, 2018) (older readers)

Town by James Roy (University of Queensland Press, 2007) (older readers)

POETRY

Children love poetry. There is something hardwired into the human brain that, independent of culture or upbringing, responds to rhyme, rhythm and words that can be memorised and chanted. Before adults overthink and panic about poetry, they should pause and recognise that it is very often the first form of text or story that we share with a young child, be it through songs or nursery rhyme.

Natalie Jane Prior is a multiple award-winning author and now a friend, and not just because she thought to include me as the image of the librarian in *Lucy's Book*, illustrated by Cheryl Orsini! *A Boat of Stars*, a poetry anthology she edited with Margaret Connelly, is a beautiful collection of accessible poems to share with the young. Natalie is the perfect person to tell us how and why to share poetry with readers young and old.

Natalie Jane Prior

Like prayer and music, poetry is primal. It's language operating simultaneously at its most fundamental and sophisticated levels. Nothing enriches a child's understanding of how language works more than poetry. Reading it teaches children to think outside the square, to see things from unexpected angles. In our modern world this skill is becoming essential. Don't think of poetry as an optional extra: think of it as a weapon in your children's arsenal for life.

Even if it's not something you're naturally drawn to yourself, teaching your children to love poetry is not as daunting as you might think. Start off by making sure that your new baby has one good quality book of nursery rhymes and one anthology of poems aimed at early childhood, and read one or two as part of the nightly bedtime routine. You'll soon find which ones are the favourites. Encourage your children to learn these by heart and recite them with you and, as they move further into the pre-reading stage, point out the rhyming words on the page so that they can associate the sounds with the letters. Move your bodies in time with the rhythm of the words as you read or recite: march and clap and bounce, and find ways of making every favourite poem your very own. Many picture books aimed at the very young are also written in verse. Some are better than others, but ALL good picture book texts depend for their success on rhythm and cadence – something that is worth playing up to when you read them aloud.

Finally, don't be afraid to experiment. When my daughter Elizabeth was small, a poem we read over and over again was 'The Night Mail' by W. H. Auden, which was written for a 1936 documentary film, for adults, about mail sorting. What was it about this poem that made it special for us? It was the rhythm of the words, mimicking the train rattling over the tracks as it sped from London to Scotland, picking up mail of all different kinds along the way. Is there a poem you are particularly fond of? If so, share it. Chances are, your children will like it, too.

Guinea Pig Town and Other Animal Poems by Lorraine Marwood (Walker Books Australia, 2013)

A Ute Picnic and Other Australian Poems by Lorraine Marwood (Walker Books Australia, 2010)

Note on the Door and Other Poems About Family Life by Lorraine Marwood (Walker Books Australia, 2011)

Love Poems and Leg Spinners by Steven Herrick (University Queensland Press, 2001)

A Boat of Stars edited by Margaret Connelly and Natalie Jane Prior (ABC Books, 2018)

A Paddock of Poems by Max Fatchen (Penguin Books Australia, 1987)

100 Australian Poems for Children edited by Clare Scott Mitchell and Kathlyn Griffith (Random House Australia, 2002)

Mongerel Doggerel by Elizabeth Honey (Allen & Unwin, 1998)

Can You Keep a Secret? edited by Mark Carthew (Random House Australia, 2008)

Untangling Spaghetti by Steven Herrick (University of Queensland Press, 2009)

VERSE NOVELS

Verse novels are narratives told in verse. They may be written in rhyme, or free verse – or include a variety of poetic forms. Some verse novels are made up of short, individual poems; others are longer, chapter-length poems. But always they tell a story: the bare bones and heart of the story without being weighed down by flesh and fat. Kat Apel is an expert verse novelist and her books are never on the shelves of my primary school library – they are constantly in the hands of young readers and as soon as they are returned they are borrowed by someone else! I love how Kat talks here about the weight of words.

Kathryn Apel

I have often thought that a poet is a combination of body-builder, topiary artist and clown, and that's especially true when writing verse novels. Every word is weighted. For each word on the page, a multitude of words has been pruned out. Yet verse novels surprise and delight with wordplay and poetic twists. They are eloquent – words seem to have more resonance. Verse novels deal with issues that have a lot of heart. They have humour and laughter too, but I think the raw emotions are key. Because they're often written in first person and because they're distilled words, you climb right inside the characters' hearts – both as writer and reader. Their heartaches become your tears, their insecurities become your introspections, their achievements become your joy.

In terms of reader-appeal I would say that verse novels are a paradox; they appeal to kids who struggle with words on the page, but also to sophisticated readers. There is often more white space than words and that makes for a clean, clear read, while the layout helps pace the poem and enhance meaning. But that doesn't dumb the reading down! Being more about emotions than details, verse novels move the story along at a swift pace. They are often very visual – in a sense, the words are the illustrations – and that opens up a whole new realm of visual literacy, with hidden layers to the text. (Kids love to discover little tricks scattered through the pages.) So they're enabling, while also being engaging.

However, I don't think I can write about verse novels without acknowledging that kids might initially be reluctant to read them. When they pick up a book and flick through it for themselves they see poems and are often hesitant to read further. (I suspect frequent analysis of poetry within the education system makes it seem arduous – when really poetry is so much fun!) So the first time your child encounters a verse novel, it might be necessary to introduce it with a shared reading: maybe lightly discuss word placement on the page, look for pictures in words, talk about rule-breakers, or how the book is making them feel. When they're engaged, you can step back and let them take over the reading – or continue reading together. I always envisaged *Bully on the Bus* as a shared reading experience between a young child and their parent or caregiver, to give young children words and open up discussions about situations where they might not feel safe. So often kids say they 'forget' a book is a verse novel and are just swept away by the story. Sometimes they just can't turn the pages fast enough! Other times they want to dwell in the words on a page; walk away and savour the feelings they create. Again, that paradox – verse novels could be read quickly, but might *need* to be read slowly.

To me, verse novels are a treasure hunt in book form. That's something we can all enjoy!

Bully on the Bus by Kathryn Apel (University of Queensland Press, 2014)

Too Many Friends by Kathryn Apel (University of Queensland Press, 2017)

On Track by Kathryn Apel (University of Queensland Press, 2015)

The Spangled Drongo by Stephen Herrick (University of Queensland Press, 1999)

Pookie Aleera Is Not My Boyfriend by Stephen Herrick (University of Queensland Press, 2012)

Tom Jones Saves the World by Stephen Herrick (University of Queensland Press, 2002)

Pearl Verses the World by Sally Murphy (Walker Books Australia, 2009)

Roses Are Blue by Sally Murphy (Walker Books Australia, 2014)

Toppling by Sally Murphy (Walker Books Australia, 2010)

Sixth Grade Style Queen (Not!) by Sherryl Clark (Penguin Books Australia, 2007)

Sister Heart by Sally Morgan (Fremantle Press, 2015)

COMICS AND GRAPHIC NOVELS

Comics and graphic novels tell stories in both visual and written form. Comics are serialised stories that are told over many editions and often many years. We get to know the characters slowly and we see different 'snapshots' of their lives. Graphic novels, on the other hand, are a single work in one book – a story from beginning to end. As the term 'graphic novel' suggests, they follow more the format and style of a novel. Graphic novels have had a phenomenal rise in popularity lately but have actually *always* been popular; it's just that they have become accepted in 'mainstream reading circles'.

Young people rely on visual media for their information and entertainment. They don't read instructions these days; instead they find someone demonstrating it on YouTube. This seems counter-intuitive to us older folk, but the visual element is crucial to the younger generation. Graphic novels often fulfil this need in their reading too. Graphic novels are not a 'dumbed down' way of reading. It takes a certain maturity and ability to decode the words and pictures simultaneously to construct meaning and follow the narrative. Japanese manga has another layer above that – a cultural awareness and appreciation for the artistic design and genre itself. Children of all ages love graphic novels and there is a steady diet of Marvel, DC, manga and novel-adapted illustrated books to suit every taste.

I met the author Stephen Axelsen at the StoryArts Festival Ipswich many moons ago. Stephen has the driest and most wicked sense of humour and I love seeing this sparkle come through in his writing and illustrations, particularly in his Piccolo and Annabelle series and his Nelly Gang graphic novels. I've asked Stephen to talk about graphic novels as I reckon he has created some of the best in the country for young people.

Stephen Axelsen

'Sequential art', 'graphic novel', 'bande dessinée' and 'comic strip' are all interchangeable descriptors for the format, to some degree. 'Sequential art' sounds technical and prissy, 'graphic novel' ponderous, 'comic strip or comic book' inaccurate because so many publications are not comedic at all. Presently I prefer the French term 'bande dessinée', 'drawn strip', both for the straightforward description of the medium and because it is French.

I love the making of strip stories as much as I do reading them – more probably. There is such a sweet marrying of picture and word, especially when doing both the writing and the illustrating. There is a kind of perpetual cross-pollination. A neat graphic idea in single frame might shift the course of a narrative, for a page or for the whole story. One bright phrase might require the scrapping of a double spread of art. Now that I think of it, some pollination instances can be quite cross-making!

The construction of framed art page is like cutting a jigsaw puzzle with a blunt jigsaw. It requires much shuffling and shaving, squeezing and stretching. Two millimetres are cut here and pasted there, to make space for an important extra word in a slightly bigger balloon. I love it when a page falls into place and the final frame leads seamlessly to the next page. The 'Turn Of Page', especially at the end of a double spread, is critical. The graphic novel provides the scope for a lot of story in a limited space. There is room for a plot and subplots for character development, for action and drama and quiet spells. There is room for a novel.

Why read graphic novels? If you are nine and books are a waste of precious time, read a graphic novel. Streams and streams of uninterrupted book words are scary. A few words within a picture are manageable bite-sized morsels. These few words are read and understood with the help of their supporting image. Each digested speech balloon is a small victory. Slowly bigger balloons are managed. The balloons drag and lift the nine-year-old child up and away, away to Dostoyevsky or some such. I have met a professional writer who taught himself to read because he absolutely had to understand what The Phantom was saying inside those balloons.

Perhaps a graphic novel does too much of the visual imagineering for the reader/watcher. Does this inhibit the development of a young person's imaginative capabilities? I don't know. This is a question for the neuropsychologists. But I strongly suspect that the exposure to really good imagery intertwined with compelling stories can only be nourishing. It still is for me. I continue to look, absorb and expand my own perceptions, skills and ambitions.

The graphic novel is not just beneficial to the reluctant reader, nor just for the adult socially inept 'geek'. At their best, the graphic novel is an art form with its own rich aesthetics. There are many and various ways the illustrations can tell a story, often with a sparse amount of text. There is a wealth of visual tools to aid in the evocation of mood and tone, pathos and drama, humour and discordance: the spacing, placing and shaping, overlapping or even absence of frames, use of colour, texture, line style (bold, broken, tremulous). In fact, the elements of any two dimensional visual art can be employed, and structured for affect in the sequence of frames.

A graphic novel can be an almost filmic experience, like seeing a movie with 90 per cent of the frames removed. But unlike a movie, the story and the art can be absorbed at leisure, re-read in bits, the illustrations lingered over. Just as the reader of an unillustrated book can admire the word craft of a fine writer, a graphic novel reader can revel and delight in the drawing and colour skills of a fine illustrator, and the wonderful innovative ways that ideas, sometimes difficult or abstract, are rendered visually. The illustrator is not an embellisher or embroiderer of words. The good illustrator is an enhancer and an augmenter (and another word that I can't think of!).

Kidglovz by Julie Hunt (Allen & Unwin, 2015)

The Mostly True Story of Matthew and Trim by Cassandra Golds, illustrated by Stephen Axelsen (Penguin, 2005)

The Arrival by Shaun Tan (Hachette Australia, 2006)

Scarygirl by Nathan Jurevicius (Allen & Unwin, 2009)

Ruben by Bruce Whatley (Scholastic Australia, 2017)

Unforgotten by Tohby Riddle (Murdoch Books, 2012)

Ubby's Underdogs by Brenton E. McKenna (Magabala Books, 2011)

The Boy, the Bear, the Baron, the Bard and Other Dramatic Tales by Gregory Rogers (Allen & Unwin, 2015)

The Nelly Gang by Stephen Axelsen (Walker Books Australia, 2013)

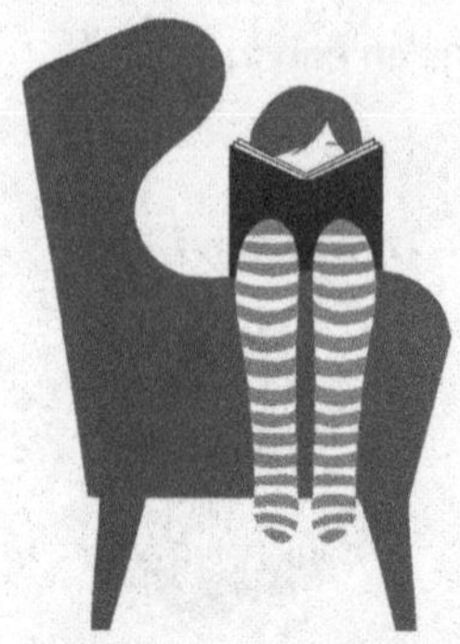

CHAPTER NINE

MULTIMODAL AND DIGITAL READING

There is an element of apprehension among parents and educators about reading in the digital age. The overwhelming perception is that young people are choosing technology over reading and online games over the worlds in books. The advent of ebooks, apps and the rise in the use of personal devices has caused waves of concern, and there is good reason to be mindful of both screen time and digital reading. However, the clock cannot be turned back to a time before technology - nor would we want it to be - so the challenge is to embrace the wonders of reading in a digital age.

Technology means we are now more connected than ever before to the stories of others, both worldwide and in our local community. In fact, we have the opportunity to expand the literary experiences of young readers beyond traditional print texts and into this digital age of reading. Rather than screen time eroding literacy rates, it could actually instigate the 'golden age of reading'. We have the opportunity to consider new ways of thinking and doing in literacy learning, if we acknowledge the richness of the digital activities in which our young people are engaged. And for those who despair the decline of 'the book' as we know it? Well, we are now some way into the digital book revolution and it seems clear that traditional print books will form part of personal and institutional libraries for the foreseeable future and will happily sit alongside ebooks and other digital reading opportunities.

Changes to the way we teach literacy are also occurring in classrooms, in response to ever-evolving digital technologies. It is timely that the challenges and implications of digital communication technologies for literacy education be considered; however, many classrooms and national standardised testing requirements are still principally focused on the reading and writing of print-based texts. The challenge for educators is to embed new ways of reading and writing into classroom planning and teaching, while holding on to the richness of experience gained from traditional print-based texts. Likewise, as parents now have access to multiple digital options with which to equip and entertain their children, many families struggle to find the right balance of screen time. Like educators, they want their children to enhance their digital skills but are concerned about how this may affect their child's engagement with print texts and their levels of literacy. They too are looking for answers as to how the various forms of reading may co-exist in a technologically complex world.

Educators talk of 'multimodal literacy' as a way of articulating the increasingly diverse forms of communicating information. Modes of reading (such as images, words, sounds, movement, tactile and spatial) may be used in combination, to make meaning when reading, comprehending and responding to various multimedia and digital texts, and in the planning, writing and producing of multimedia and digital texts.[1] Multimodal texts include picture books, graphic novels, some ebooks and visuals like posters, where meaning is made by combining visual images, text and spatial modes. Digital multimodal texts include web pages, social media, apps, animations, films and some ebooks and online gaming tools, where meaning is made through spoken language, visual (still and moving), audio, gestural, written and spatial modes. And finally, 'real-life' multimodal text experiences include performance, song, storytelling, some online gaming tools and dance. Modes such as images, words, sounds and movement in a text may be processed by the reader simultaneously or one mode may dominate. For example, the reading of a picture book will be dominated by the visual mode and in listening to an audio book the mode of sound will be dominant.

Digital technologies have enabled rapid changes in the way young people learn to read and become literate, hence the focus on multiple ways of reading or 'multimodal reading'. This chapter will examine ways of incorporating multimodal reading into your homes and classrooms. It will give you the tools to embrace, or at least work with, new and ever-evolving digital technologies. Special thanks for expert advice in this chapter must go to Jackie Child, digital technologies educator, teacher librarian and author of the respected blog *TinkeringChild*.

TURN THEM INTO EXPERTS FIRST!

Familiarise your young reader with their technology and have them develop their expertise so they are not reliant on adults to use their digital device or online reading mode of choice. This may seem ridiculous in a world where teachers and parents often bemoan the fact that 'the young people' navigate new technologies with seeming ease and grace. However, often their level of expertise is related to what results in the fastest outcome for them, not necessarily how to use the technology for maximum academic or social benefit. Jackie Child has developed many units of work around digital technologies which often start with skill development, whether it be for a particular app, a new brand of robotics equipment or a 'new to them' coding program. It is important to find the balance between playful independent exploration of technology and planned, sequential and specific skill development. As an example, when introducing e-readers into our school library collection some years ago, we planned and taught a unit of work in which we developed skills in using e-readers before actually loaning them to students. As an additional benefit, teachers learnt alongside their students how to use this 'new to them' technology. We demonstrated basic skills such as using the dictionary, adding notes, highlighting and inserting bookmarks. We looked at and brainstormed reasons why customised reading on an e-reader may be of benefit, changing the font size, background colours, text-to-audio function and page layout. Importantly we also learnt about the hardware and how to care for it, charge it and troubleshoot problems and, finally, we signed 'user agreement' forms around care of the devices and appropriate use. This resulted in higher levels of expertise and, consequently, changed the social dynamic in the classroom, as the teachers were no longer the sole providers of knowledge, with the students becoming skilled experts in the use of these particular devices.

CODING – THE 'NEW LITERACY'

The 'science of computers' offers not just an understanding of hardware and software, but a framework for thinking, often called 'computational thinking'. Computational thinking refers to looking at a problem in a way that a computer does. It involves thinking logically, decomposing into smaller parts, looking for and recognising patterns, abstracting ideas, designing algorithms and making judgements. It may sound a bit like learning to read because it is very similar. Coding is a language, with variables and rules that govern it, just like the language of words, hence coding being referred to as a 'new' form of literacy.

We communicate with a computer through coding (or programming) and it is important we give children the opportunity to learn to read and write code, just as we do with music, dance and sport. Not all children will be musicians or athletes but the experience of these activities helps in developing a well-rounded child and the skills they develop stay with them through life. There are many children for whom coding is a passion and they may want to further develop skills in computer science. Text coding (or programming) can be quite complex for younger students to grasp, but with a visual programming language such as Scratch or Blockly students can learn to write code and then progress onto text-based programming like Java or Python.

When students are learning to code either through online programs or with devices like robots, they are developing skills in tinkering (playing and inventing), creating (by designing and making), debugging (finding and fixing), persevering, risk-taking and collaborating.

Computers touch our lives in so many ways, from movies to medicine, education to entertainment, gaming to government, construction to commerce. It was just a few centuries ago when only the elite and religious could communicate through writing and reading. With computers dominating nearly every aspect of our lives, it is vital we have students who can create and instruct these digital technologies using coding skills. This 'new literacy' of coding enables students to not just use digital technologies, but to read, comprehend and create them.

COMPUTATIONAL THINKING AND CODING BOOKS FOR BEGINNERS AND YOUNG READERS

Hello Ruby: Adventures in coding (and others in the series) by Linda Liukas (Puffin Books, 2016)

Ada Byron Lovelace and the Thinking Machine by Laurie Wallmark, illustrated by April Chu (Creston Books, 2015)

If I Were a Wizard by Paul Hamilton, illustrated by Simon Howe (Paul Hamilton, 2017)

Lift-the-Flap Coding and Computers (and others in the series) by Rosie Dickins, illustrated by Shaw Nielsen (Usborne, 2015)

Beginner's Guide to Coding by Marc Scott, illustrated by Mick Marston (Bloomsbury, 2016)

Computational Fairy Tales (and others in the series) by Jeremy Kubica (CreateSpace, 2012)

DK Coding Workbooks by DK and Jon Woodcock (Dorling Kindersley, 2015)

HTML for Babies (and others in series) by John Vanden-Heuvel (Sterling Children's Books, 2016)

EBOOKS

Nothing can replace the tactile nature of a print book and the importance of young children learning to turn a page and work out what is the front cover, back cover, spine and endpapers. Equally, there is something to be said for the persistence it takes for a newly confident reader to sustain reading from start to finish of a book without hyperlinking out, clicking on pop-ups or swiping from side to side.

However, digital devices for reading have much to offer. Good literary apps and worthy ebooks do an amazing job engaging readers, particularly those who are unable to sustain attention for an entire print book or those who need to 'read' while moving (hello toddlers, sporty types and fidgeters of all ages). They also allow slightly older readers to delve deeper into a book, clicking on an author bio, navigating to the dictionary to find out the meaning of an unknown word or downloading the next book in a series immediately, in order to keep up the reading momentum. While ebook readers tend to replicate a print-text reading experience, for some young readers, ebooks have opened up the world of story in a way that was not possible before, through varied screen size options, page-turning features, and general layout, as well as many tools and settings (including audio narration) which allow for a wide range of individualised reading experiences.[2]

Family friends have a ten-year-old daughter who was gifted an e-reading device for her birthday, along with gift cards for the purchasing of ebooks. Her reading rate and fluency has increased exponentially, and it has given her a sense autonomy and responsibility in her choices as she can access books at the touch of a button wherever she is. She has become incredibly adept at leaving succinct yet insightful reviews on titles she has purchased and she now requests further gift cards for ebooks as gifts or pocket money. I see this as a gentle introduction (always monitored by parents) to the world of digital technologies and the responsibilities that go along with such a privilege. Book choices need to be responsible, safety measures need to be considered when commenting on or reviewing books, pop-ups need to be read with a critical eye, and a budget for books needs to be considered with transactions that occur digitally. Well before your child enters the world of social media, ebook reading can provide a sense of 'dipping your toe' into the puddle that is the internet.

APPS

There is a wealth of book apps available (most existing also as print books) and young children are adept at engaging with story apps and the interactive features and learning tools they offer. In print-based texts, children experience narratives in a linear fashion, whereas digital texts, in particular game-based apps, put the child firmly in the centre of the action and allow them to manipulate and even rewrite the narrative. When print and digital combine it is a total story experience and a perfect example of multimodal reading in action.

There are book apps for a range of reading ages and stages and some, such as the *Animalia* app (based on *Animalia* by Graeme Base) or the *Hairy Maclary* app (based on the series by Lynley Dodd), will engage multiple generations of readers, with many parents having grown up with print versions of these books. Apps based on books have the ability to extend the reading experience, creating a sense of interactivity that is often unable to be achieved through the reading of a print book. Young app users may be able to navigate their own path through the story, in some cases manipulating the narrative structure. They may hone in on a particular character and learn more about them, have a story read aloud to them, or enjoy sound effects or music which accompanies a story. They may even be invited to be co-creators in the reading/writing experience, and they are often able to respond to a text in a digitally creative manner.

The very best book-based apps still keep *story* as the central focus, allowing readers to follow and enjoy the basic narrative structure of the original book but adding in the right balance of special effects and changeable elements. Simply adding interaction and sound to a book does not create the ideal app and, in many cases, the book would have been best left alone. As the possibilities of the technologies become apparent, more well-established authors and illustrators are working with highly skilled app developers to design original books apps that make best use of the technology, rather than simply converting existing books to app form. A recent example of this is *Paperbark*. As users meander mindfully through an Australian bush setting illustrated by author/illustrator Renee Treml, they become part of a beautiful short story about a wombat who spends his days exploring and foraging through the bush as he searches for a new home. Users can click on and learn more about plant species and threats to native animals, or simply enjoy the immersive experience as the Australian landscape is brought to life through vibrant watercolours and sounds. Book or story apps for children and teens like *Paperbark* enrich the literary experience for young people, taking full advantage of technical functionality such as animation, interactivity and gamification to engage, educate and entertain.

There are also apps which can be used in conjunction with books, with augmented reality and virtual reality elements now being incorporated into some traditional print books. This technology promotes interaction with the book in the real world and opens infinite possibilities to various realities for young readers. Longstanding favourite books like The Guinness World Record series now invite readers to scan a QR code and interact with online content as they read. There are also many apps which invite the reader to become an author in the digital environment. Apps such as *Book Creator* allow even very young children to create digital books and develop their own stories. Recently a prep student I teach spent her holidays writing and illustrating a story in paper form but she then decided she wanted to share it with a wider audience. She and her mother investigated together how to convert her illustrations to digital form and create a simple digital story. The book was then 'advertised' to friends and family via social media and many purchased, read and provided encouragement on her work, creating an authentic audience for this budding writer.

AUDIO BOOKS

Children's books in audio form are a great way for kids to experience stories in an aural mode. Audio books have similar benefits to being read aloud to, with audio books considered an important tool in literacy development.[3] Some people view audio books as the 'easy' option for young people, but as part of a balanced literary diet they greatly enrich the reading experience, and many of the skills and strategies used are comparable to reading a visual text. They also help to develop attention and listening skills and many children who are unable to make it through a long children's book will make it through the same story in audio, carried along by the sound effects, accompanying music, and expressive voices of actors and storytellers.

Audio books can also help to introduce children to text which is above their reading level, particularly when a child is following along with the print version and is hearing the words while seeing the shape of them on the page. The expressive voices of the professional narrator provides a fluid reading of a text which presents proper use of punctuation and cadence.[4]

For ESL students, students with sight difficulties, low interest readers and children who are unable to read print or settle to reading for a variety of reasons, audio books remove barriers to story. Taking away the mechanics of reading texts enables children to visualise the story, the setting and the characters in their head. A love of reading can be sparked when a child finds an audio book they love and the print copy of the book is introduced when they are ready.

For me, the wonder of audio books is how portable they are with one digital device providing countless hours of story. Commuting to sport, school, holiday destinations or the shops can be made so much more enjoyable with a great audio book and the entire family can engage simultaneously and discuss it at length.

ONLINE STORYBOOK READINGS

Here I am not advocating readings of books on YouTube by individuals who neither credit nor pay the original creators of the book and which are often poor quality recordings of loved stories. There are, however, a number of online streaming services that are subscription-based and often available for free through council libraries. Story readings by professional actors or expert readers connect children with literature through the complementary mode of film, again creating a multimodal reading experience.

I use one such subscription-based service, Story Box Library, at home and in the classroom, and for the past few years I have made good use of it in the lead-up to Anzac Day, because it has a beautiful collection of Anzac Day stories exquisitely read aloud. While I love reading aloud to my own children and to my students at school, the Story Box Library's readings offer students a variety of voices and storytelling techniques. I cannot watch *I Was Only Nineteen* read by John Schumann without ending up in tears. The warmth with which John reads this powerful book is heartfelt and he introduces it standing in front of Melbourne's Shrine of Remembrance - not something I can re-create in real life. Likewise, I will never be able to read a book like *One Minute's Silence* (by David Metzenthen and Michael Camilleri) as emotively as actor Shane Jacobson. The reading by Tiffany Speight of *Anzac Biscuits* by Phil Cummings again gives students a context for the story which I cannot provide in a school library. Tiffany is seated in a country kitchen and the filming switches between the book and the kitchen, where Anzac biscuits are being made. The visuals invite young viewers into the setting of the story from the comfort of their library or home and adds a whole other dimension to the book.

GAMING

Online gaming is widespread among tweens and teens and many parents and educators despair at the hours that can be lost in these online worlds. However, for many young people, gaming is a space in which they experience success, sustained and pleasurable entertainment and a sense of control and independence over their environment. Online gaming can also serve as a rich source of storytelling and story-creating, imaginative growth and connectedness with peers online and offline.

Gaming requires high levels of literacy and comprehension: the ability to follow complex narratives, the skills to synthesise multiple modes of reading, the need to read deeply and think critically to solve complex problems and the mechanical literacy to navigate a gaming environment, make quick decisions under pressure, and skim, scan and decode fast-moving text and images. Gaming also often requires a high level of written ability through responding to comments from other players, coding avatars, and contributing hacks and critiques to gaming sites. Our challenge is to harness these positives and engage young people in meaningful ways with other forms of literacy learning. If young people are motivated to read the complex text of a game, we can transfer that motivation to a book through careful text selection: the right book at the right time for the right child.

Spin-off books from popular online gaming sites are common and these books may engage young people in reading, if the text is of a high standard and employs the same engaging tone as the game on which it is based. Seeking out a series with similar concepts to favourite games, such as those with complex physical challenges, good versus evil plotlines, or stories of survival of the fittest, can engage keen gamers in traditional print books.

Popular fantasy series of books often have fan sites similar to gaming sites. Many readers greatly enjoy the sense of connectedness they feel from finding people who love similar books, and gamers are familiar with interacting on fan sites. Online gaming worlds are complex places and the sense of setting is key to engaging players and keeping them 'in' the world. Seek books with complex worlds, maps and a strong sense of place. Follow online interests and use comparative texts to write critiques or innovate on a text/game by adding new characters or changing endings. Reflect on the ethical dilemmas faced in games and seek books with similarly complex ethical issues such as The Hunger Games series (Suzanne Collins), Deltora Quest series (Emily Rodda) or The Mortal Instruments series (Cassandra Clare).

DIGITAL LITERATURE

More and more we are seeing masterful pieces of digital literature which combine narrative, non-fiction, poetry or graphic novel style writing with the latest technological innovations. I am not talking here about books that have been converted to digital, such as ebooks, but works of contemporary writing that have been designed specifically to be consumed by readers in digital form. This may seem a step too far for some parents, educators and young readers but, to me, they are an example of everything that is great about the smash-up that is happening between technology and books. Digital literature takes the very best of technology and combines it with the wonder of prose and we are really only at the beginnings of the possibilities for this emerging area of contemporary literature.

The most well-known example to many middle readers and Australian educators is *Inanimate Alice*, a Bradfield Company Production (2005–2018), and *Inanimate Alice: Perpetual Nomads*, an international co-production between Bradfield Narrative Design and Mez Breeze Design. The series is multi-award-winning and in 2012 it was named Best Website for Teaching and Learning by the American Association of School Librarians. The Year Five teachers at school have been using *Inanimate Alice* since 2013 as a unit of work in English and Digital Technologies. The student goals for this unit of work include:

- apply critical and creative literacy skills to deconstruct digital fiction texts as readers
- analyse and establish author's craft, purpose and formulas
- write and create their own digital text
- reflect critically on their own role as readers and writers throughout this digital storytelling journey
- develop critical literacy skills to compare and contrast strategies used when reading and writing printed and digital text types.

DIGITAL READS

Our Cupidity Coda by Mez Breeze (http://mezbreezedesign.com/vr-literature/our-cupidity-coda/)

A Place Called Ormalcy by Mez Breeze (http://mezbreezedesign.com/vr-literature/a-place-called-ormalcy/)

Little Emperor Syndrome by David Thomas Henry Wright, with Chris Arnold (http://www.littleemperorsyndrome.com/)

Core Values by Benjamin Laird (https://poetry.codetext.net/core-values/)

CRITICAL LITERACY SKILLS

At the start of this chapter I talked about the importance of up-skilling students in the use of devices. Equally as important is equipping them with skills to critically analyse a multimodal text by evaluating:

- the credibility/quality of the texts (that is, who is producing them?)
- the commercialisation that comes with accessing multimodal texts online (for example, advertising, hyperlinking to promote other texts, in-app purchases, etc)
- the appropriate ways to use content in the creation of their own multimodal texts, for example, copyright laws – how many times do we teachers need to talk to students about using copyright-free images and music (bangs head against classroom wall)?

There is no doubt that technology-infused experiences of literacy are reshaping learning environments and the contemporary reading practices of children. Older generations did not have to contend with the constant movement between modes and media which children nowadays need to efficiently manage to create meaning from texts. While we may look on with concern, there appears to be as many benefits as there are drawbacks. It is an exciting time as we meld the old with the new, print with digital.

What is apparent is that for students to tap into the potential advantages of digital reading, they need new skills and strategies to successfully use and adapt to the rapidly changing information and communication technologies and contexts. Digital literacy is ever-evolving, and the challenge for educators and parents is to transform reading instruction and experiences in response to emerging technologies and new possibilities for communication and collaboration.

CHAPTER TEN

READING THE VISUALS

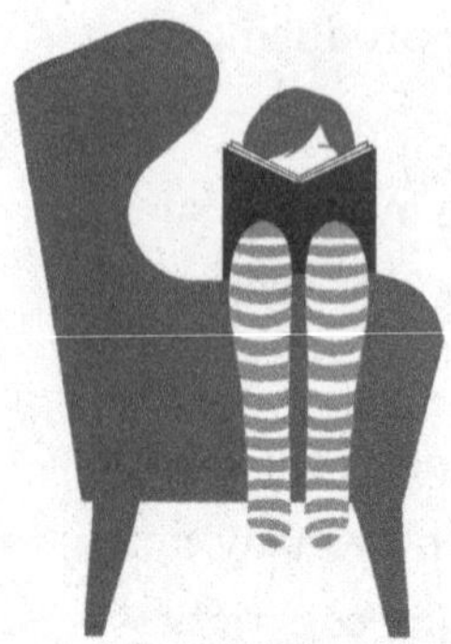

Why anyone would want to leave picture books behind is beyond me. They are works of art and the best way I know to enhance and teach visual literacy. The language in picture books is often complex and the storylines sophisticated and thought-provoking. So why is it that so many parents and educators 'celebrate' a child's move into chapter book territory and then actively discourage the borrowing of picture books? I wish I could say I've seen it only once, but over the years I've seen several versions of certificates handed out to young children with words similar to 'I've graduated from picture books!' I want this chapter to celebrate illustrated children's literature rather than dwell on negatives, but it is important to take a moment to examine why the perception is that illustrated texts are only for the very young.

When I talk at conferences, libraries or bookstores about the importance of picture books I often hold up my favourite one from my childhood, *Little Cloud* by Robert Tallon. I use it as an example of how picture books have changed since our childhood, although in fairness to Tallon it's actually a rather a good book and I can still recite the whole thing by heart so it clearly had an impact on me.

Like *Little Cloud*, many picture books of our childhood had beautiful but fairly simple illustrations, mostly a front view of the character and the setting. Illustrations often existed to merely capture and reinforce what was said in the text. The language was at a level that would have been considered appropriate for a three- or four-year-old, and the storylines often offered a moral lesson or described a simple family occasion. In both overt and subtle ways, picture books were used as a reflection of the expectations and aspirations of society at the time as well as to educate and entertain. I'm certain that many of us have held fast to our pre-conceived notions of picture books formed in our childhood, and, for the most part, have not had exposure to the richness of contemporary illustrated texts. Work your way through the lists at the end of this chapter and I guarantee you will be converted!

Of course, it is a generalisation that all older picture books are simplistic in nature, with books by Ida Rentoul Outhwaite, Norman Lindsay, May Gibbs, Jenny Wagner and Ron Brooks immediately springing to mind as examples to the contrary. The State Library of Victoria houses over 100,000 Australian and international children's books in the Children's Literature Collection which showcases the wonder of Australian children's illustrated works from the early nineteenth century to the twenty-first century. The illustrations in this collection reflect society at different points throughout history and many are fine examples of art at its very best.

PICTURE BOOKS

When I am reading and working with picture books at home with my own children and at school in library lessons, I always talk about the book as a whole, and follow a similar routine in each picture book session with students from kindergarten to Year Six. It may seem ridiculous to some that I have taken the time to outline 'how to read a picture book', but I firmly believe that so much visual literacy and other learning is embedded in picture books and it seems such a shame to miss any of it. Of course, not every picture book reading should be a formal lesson, and at all times enjoyment of the story should be paramount.

Doing picture books well

Always read a book before you share it with an individual or group of students. Every time I am tempted to grab the closest book and read it to a group of rowdy three-year-olds to calm them down, I remember The Grandparent's Day Incident of 1999. I was teaching Year Two and I grabbed a picture book about grandparents from the shelf to read to my class and the thirty or so grandparents present. The teacher librarian had helpfully put together a selection at my request. Halfway through reading the book, I realised that grandad was going to die. I kept going until I knew things were about to decline for grandad and then I shut the book and cheerily said, 'And if you want to read the rest of the book, you can visit the school library!' then announced more loudly than was necessary (lest any child ask a question about grandad in the book) that scones with jam and cream were about to be served. A grandfather sidled up to me at morning tea with a smirk on his face, and said, 'Grandad died, right?' Always pre-read a book for content!

I start most picture book readings with a good look at and discussion of the physical features of a book, explicitly pointing them out and naming them. We then make predictions about what the text might be about and how the design features help us to form an idea about the book.

Physical parts of a picture book: how and what to discuss

Title: typography size, shape, colour and size

Front and back covers: what information is contained on each? On the front cover look at the title and locate the author's and illustrator's name. If the book is from a library, can you see the library barcode? On the back cover, read the blurb, find the ISBN and any other text which identifies the publisher. Is there a photograph of the author and a bio or is this inside the book?

Spine: just like the spine in your body, the spine on a book holds the book straight and together. Also, like your own spine, the book spine needs to be treated with care and respect or we end up with a wibbly wobbly book. If the book is from a library, is there a call number sticker on the spine and what information is on this? Is the title of the book written on the spine? Why is it written in a certain direction?

Endpapers: endpapers are the pages at the start and finish of a hardcover book. They consist of a double page folded, with one half pasted to the inside cover and the other serving as the first free page. Essentially, they strengthen the book but of course they really are so much more than this! There are social media accounts dedicated to endpaper design, and astute readers know that the story in a Bob Graham book almost always begins and ends on the endpapers. I myself loudly proclaim every year to the little people at school that when I am a grown-up I am going to own an endpaper art gallery.

Other physical features include: dust jacket, double-page spread, gutter, recto/verso pages. Also consider if there are any unusual design features such as cut pages, pockets, flaps, deckle edges or fore-edge painting.

Reading a picture book: when reading a picture book for the first time I don't stop and start while I am reading to discuss a point. I read the entire text in one fluid and expressive reading. With young students I often begin by saying, 'I'm going to read you the words in this book now and your job is to listen and also to read the pictures.' In this way I make it clear that reading the visuals is as much part of a picture book as reading the text is.

On a second and sometimes third (or more) re-reading we will stop along the way and unpack ideas about the intent of the author and illustrator and how they may have used point of view, lines and colours, angles and typography to influence how we read the text. We might consider if the text and images are telling a different or parallel story and we always mull over how the book makes us feel.

VISUAL LITERACY

We access visuals continuously throughout our day, whether browsing the internet or other computer programs, in advertisements via screens and billboards, on the box of your organic granola, the artwork on the wall in your local coffee shop, and so the list goes on. Spend five or so minutes pondering the visuals you have consumed today and the messages that each artist is trying to convey and you'll soon be acutely aware that we live in an age saturated by visuals. Visual literacy then is the term used to describe the skills needed to comprehend, create and communicate with visuals.[1] While text-based literacy instruction is considered essential, visual literacy does not receive the same level of attention in educational settings, although there has recently been a renewed focus. The Australian Curriculum recognises the importance of visuals in literacy and meaning-making, and each year level now has content descriptors which detail how students are expected to learn in relation to visual literacy.

Visual language features: how and what to discuss

There are countless visual language features to discuss when viewing a picture book and a few are outlined in detail below. Also consider other features such as the use of media, the design and layout of a page or an entire book and the angles an illustrator has chosen.[2]

Lines and vectors (action and direction of lines or lines formed by shapes): discuss what sort of lines you see in the images of a picture book. Are the lines formed by the shapes of objects? Are they straight or curved? Could the lines be changed in style and still retain meaning? Do the lines take your eye to a particular part of the illustration? Are there intersecting lines and do they cross at a particular point in the image? Do the outlines of the characters lend a particular mood or feeling - contrast here the open and free lines of the work of Ann James in *I'm a Hungry Dinosaur* (written by Janeen Brian) with the sharp black lines used by Jules Faber in the illustrations in the WeirDo series (written by Anh Do). Find some examples of vectors in picture books - *Sorry Day* by Coral Vass and Dub Leffler, for example - and have children identify the movement and direction which the vectors force in the viewer.

Colour: colour can be symbolic or used to represent a feeling or mood. It can be used sparingly to great effect or splashed boldly to create a different sense. Different colours evoke different feelings and are often dependent on cultural and historical contexts - for example, Western cultures often use black to represent death whereas many Asian countries use white. The use of red in *And the Ocean Was Our Sky* (Patrick Ness, illustrated by Rovina Cai) and in *Swan Lake* (Anne Spudvilas) are fine examples of colour as strong element of visual literacy. What does the red represent in each of these books? Consider what red might represent in another context - love or passion, for example; or good luck in a Chinese text. Look at a colour wheel and the spectrum of colours on it - what feelings do these colours evoke in you? Can you find books with similar colours and feelings? Can you find an example of a warm-toned book and a cool-toned book?

Symbols: symbols and signs are like a text abbreviation and they may represent something from somewhere else (say a symbol from a well-known fairytale). They may also include icons, such as the Opera House to represent a story being set in Sydney without direct mention of the city. Can you see any symbols? Do they represent a place? A concept? A feeling (a heart, for example)? Impending danger for a character? Look carefully at the symbols in *Claris: The Chicest Mouse in Paris* (Megan Hess) and make a list of them. What do they represent? What feeling about Claris is the author trying to elicit in the reader?[3]

Point of view: authors and illustrators position a reader to see subjects and add feelings to the story based on placement; for example, placing a subject down low and looking up can create a feeling of being small and insignificant. Sometimes we are positioned as readers looking in at the action front on and other times we are placed as a character and experience the book from a different point of view. How are you positioned to view the image? How does the choice of distance affect how you feel? Do you feel part of the action or isolated? Alone or part of a group? Why has the illustrator made this choice? Why might a bird's-eye view be used? Can you find an example of this? Why might a direct gaze be used? How does it make you feel to be up close to a direct gaze?

PICTURE BOOKS AS VISUAL LITERACY TEACHING TOOLS

This list could be extensive – these are just a few that I consider 'must-haves' in talking about the elements of visual literacy with young people.

Look, A Book by Libby Gleeson, illustrated by Freya Blackwood (Hardie Grant Egmont, 2017)

Ruben by Bruce Whatley (Scholastic Australia, 2017)

Lucky by David Mackintosh (Harper Collins, 2015)

Rules of Summer by Shaun Tan (Lothian, 2013)

Cicada by Shaun Tan (Lothian, 2018)

Midnight at the Library by Ursula Dubosarsky, illustrated by Ron Brooks (National Library of Australia Publishing, 2018)

Swan Lake by Anne Spudvilas (Allen & Unwin, 2017)

The Incredible Freedom Machines by Kirli Saunders, illustrated by Matt Ottley (Scholastic Australia, 2018)

WORDLESS PICTURE BOOKS AS VISUAL LITERACY TEACHING TOOLS

Far from being books for the very young, wordless picture books are sophisticated visual narratives that are often aimed at much older readers. They invite discussion and are perfect when practising 'reading the visuals'.

The Lion and the Mouse by Jerry Pinkney (Little Brown, 2009)

A Ball for Daisy by Chris Raschka (Schwartz and Wade, 2011)

The Arrival by Shaun Tan, (Lothian Children's Books, 2006).

Anno's Italy by Mitsumasa Anno (Philomel Books, 1978)

Mirror by Jeannie Baker (Candlewick Press, 2010)

Journey by Aaron Becker (Candlewick Press, 2013)

The Snowman by Raymond Briggs (Penguin, 2002)

Unspoken: A Story from the Underground Railroad by Henry Cole (Scholastic Press, 2012)

The Middle Passage: White Ships/Black Cargo by Tom Feelings (Dial Books, 1995)

Sidewalk Circus by Paul Fleischman (Candlewick Press, 2007)

The Red Wheelbarrow by Briony Stewart (University of Queensland Press, 2012)

Flora and the Flamingo by Molly Idle (Chronicle Books, 2013)

Wave by Suzy Lee (Chronicle Books, 2008)

The Red Book by Barbara Lehman (Houghton Mifflin, 2004)

Rainstorm by Barbara Lehman (Houghton Mifflin, 2007)

The Secret Box by Barbara Lehman (Houghton Mifflin, 2011)

Chalk by Bill Thomson (Marshall Cavendish, 2010)

Flotsam by David Wiesner (Clarion, 2006)

ILLUSTRATED CHAPTER BOOKS AS VISUAL LITERACY TEACHING TOOLS

The following is not an extensive list but a starting point for sharing illustrated chapter books with young readers. These books are as much about the words as the pictures and require the reader to actively participate to make meaning.

Treehouse series by Andy Griffiths, illustrated by Terry Denton (Pan Macmillan Australia)

Samurai vs Ninja series by Nick Falk, illustrated by Tony Flowers (Penguin Random House)

How to Stop an Alien Invasion using Shakespeare and *How to Beat Genghis Khan in an Arm Wrestle* by Nick Falk, illustrated by Tony Flowers (Penguin Random House, 2016)

Anders and the Comet series by Gregory Mackay (Allen & Unwin)

Eric Vale series by Michael Gerard Bauer, illustrated by Joe Bauer (Scholastic Australia)

Big Nate series by Lincoln Pierce (Harper Collins)

Diary of a Wimpy Kid series by Jeff Kinney (Penguin Random House)

Flora and Ulysses by Kate DiCamillo, illustrated by K. G. Campbell (Candlewick Press, 2013)

Bad Guys series by Aaron Blabey (Scholastic Australia)

The skills associated with visual literacy are ones to be developed; parents, carers and educators who share picture books with young people will have witnessed firsthand the major role that visuals have in the development of a story and in the child comprehending a text.[4] In illustrated books there is a synergy between the text and images, which may not always immediately evident, due to masterful interweaving of the separate components. Careful attention to visual literacy techniques enables readers to become astute consumers and creators of images in an age where we are required to read visuals in all areas of our lives.

CHAPTER ELEVEN

READING FOR THE FUTURE – SUSTAINABILITY AND NATURE

Connecting sustainable futures and nature with reading books makes common sense if we want our young people to be engaged and receive a well-rounded education. There are few things better than seeing children get grubby in the garden, enjoying the natural world around them and learning about how to care for the earth. Observing bees, collecting leaves, inspecting insects and making mud pies is an essential part of childhood and I have very rarely encountered a child who does not enjoy pottering around in nature. Likewise, I have rarely (ever?) encountered a child who does not enjoy a quality book that is the right fit for them. While not all children have equal access to beautiful natural environments, a keen interest in sustainability and nature can be piqued early in a child's life with the right books and experiences.

Life on earth is at a critical period and there is increasing concern that we are not living within the capacity of our planet's resources. Quality books can help to put the issues in context and be a catalyst for positive change in ourselves and our young readers. They can provide a sense of hope and joy about the environment and our ability to 'make a difference'.

The importance of being in, learning about and having fun in nature is not a new concept, but the word 'sustainability' is a reasonably modern term, and the meaning is not always clear. A simple definition for sustainability might be 'enough for all, forever'. I like this way of thinking about sustainability because it includes the idea that we need to look after the planet and its resources for future generations and share it with all people in the world. It also suggests that we need to live our lives with a sense of social justice and fairness. More broadly, our society relies upon the natural environment – therefore sustainability is ultimately about supporting nature to provide us with what we need. It is about changing our behaviour to better manage resources and environmental services, so they can be sustained into the future. This may not be immediately obvious, but sustainability is also about creating an awareness of the link between the resources and environmental services we use and the natural systems that support them. These are big concepts for young children (and for adults) but kids understand about sharing, and research tells us that they are very capable of taking action for sustainability.

So when is the right time to introduce young children to environmental concerns and the concept of living sustainably? I have seen firsthand that even the youngest of children are able to grasp principles of sustainability: being mindful to dispose waste responsibly, understanding that their fruit scraps can be composted or given to the worms and knowing that insects should be returned to their habitat after inspecting them. Many young children will also have overheard discussions in the house or on the television about the effects of droughts, floods, pollution, poverty, conflict or other real-world environmental and social issues. Educating children with the help of age-appropriate books about the environmental and social challenges facing the planet need not be doom and gloom; rather, it can be a joyous way to empower young people to become problem solvers and action takers in looking after our planet. There are books on nature and sustainability aimed at children from birth, and embedding these books into all stages of childhood and into classrooms is common sense. An educational community that thrives is one where parents, students and staff work towards common goals for the good of the students and improved learning outcomes. There can be no greater goal than a school going slowly and steadily down the path to more sustainable and socially just practices resulting in a learning environment that is clean, green, innovative, community-focused and inspiring a lifelong love of the environment.

There are any number of fact books specifically on environmental issues and while these are useful, I believe there is much to be gained from stories and non-fiction texts where sustainability and nature themes are woven through a broader narrative: Like honey, stories are sticky and their concepts tend to get stuck in your mind more than isolated facts. Few children (or adults) are going to fall in love with a book that lists information about household recycling, but when a favourite character is on a 'fraught with challenges' mission to make her mother recycle the milk cartons, that story and the emotions felt will stick in the minds of young and old alike.

In Australia, the Environment Award for Children's Literature lists of winners and shortlisted titles are a good place to start when developing your collection of books supporting sustainability. The Wilderness Society manages this award because they see that children's books can have a profound effect on young people in shaping the adults they become. They seek to award books that promote a love of nature, sense of caring for the world and curiosity in children. Similarly, the Commonwealth Scientific and Industrial Research Organisation (CSIRO), an independent Australian government agency responsible for scientific research, has a well-respected publishing program which includes children's books with a focus on environmental science, aquatic science, plant and animal sciences and natural history.

Dr Lyndal O'Gorman is a senior lecturer in the School of Early Childhood and Inclusive Education, Faculty of Education, at the Queensland University of Technology in Brisbane. Her university teaching focuses on arts and sustainability education in early childhood and primary school contexts and her research and writing also explores these topics. Lyndal worked as an early childhood teacher in urban and remote schools for thirteen years prior to her academic career and has a strong personal commitment to the arts, and environmental and social sustainability.

Dr Lyndal O'Gorman

For thousands of years, the arts have played an important role in highlighting social and environmental issues. The first Australians painted and carved images of their world at least 40,000 years ago. In 1937, Picasso's painting 'Guernica' brought the horrors of the Spanish civil war to the world's consciousness and the work has since become a symbol of peace. Contemporary American artist Chris Jordan's website presents dozens of mind-blowing and confronting images that challenge us to consider humanity's impact on the planet. Mysterious British street artist Banksy's images pop up all over the world on city walls, challenging viewers to explore tough questions about social justice. The saying 'a picture paints a thousand words' communicates how powerfully art can change the ways in which we see the world. And now, more than ever, the world needs us to change the way we see it and live in it and advocate for it.

It's vital that adults who live and work with young children consider their own attitudes and preconceived ideas about sustainability. Is sustainability going to be just an interesting topic to explore and a chance to learn a little about the birds and the bees (and the worms!) or are we willing to challenge ourselves to think about what 'enough for all, forever' might really mean for our own patterns of behaviour? If we are passionate about leaving the planet in better shape for future generations, we need to live consciously now and advocate for the natural world of which we are a part, and then children will catch that passion too.

Artwork in galleries, picture books and even on the street can help children to learn about the social and natural world and the challenge of living sustainably. These days it's all but impossible for even very young children to avoid seeing confronting images. The news is full of footage of children living in poverty, or in their war-ravaged homes far away, or of wildlife and natural places that are affected by pollution and other forms of human activity. Children can use their own art to make their learning about sustainability visible to those around them. They often know more than we think they know! And art can be a language for children to use to express their thoughts and feeling about big ideas. When adults give children time and space for conversations about big issues, to engage with literature that explores those ideas, and opportunities to make their learning visible through talk and artmaking, I believe amazing things can happen.

For example, if a child has time to look at a leaf and to draw that leaf from observation, she learns to appreciate it. Appreciating the leaf leads to love, and love leads to a desire to protect – the leaf ... the tree ... the forest. I believe that sustainability is not something one 'does' for 30 minutes on a Wednesday afternoon. When we spend meaningful time with children we are in the privileged position of helping them to see the world differently – whether the world is a leaf, or a compost bin or a community in another part of the world, far from view. Children's literature can be a fabulous starting point for conversations about sustainability and social justice because literature helps us to see the world from another perspective, and therefore to see the world in new ways. These new perspectives can lead to a desire in even young children to take action so that there might be enough, for all, forever.

The amazing thing about sustainability education is that just as we are helping children to see the world differently, we see the world differently too. This knowledge can change us forever – in ways that make the planet a better place for us and for those who are to come.

READING SUPPORTING SUSTAINABILITY

Stories are the best way I know to engage children in learning and encourage behavioural change - there is nothing like having your four-year-old tell you sternly that you have not put the yoghurt container in the recycling bin! This is what nearly all sustainability and nature themed books aspire to do: to engage the reader in a particular topic so that they learn something new and/or change their behaviour, and ideally the behaviour of those around them. Many a government has tried (and failed at times) to elicit behavioural change at huge economic cost and whilst recycling may largely be a success story, we have many more challenges and opportunities for further changing how we sustain and live with the natural world. This is where literature and reading are of invaluable importance. For our children they provide inspiration, adventure in wild places and new ideas, but for our local communities and society more broadly they provide critical thinking of how we live.

When we combine real-life experiences with literature, we see great outcomes and learning in action, something we strive for in educational settings. A few years ago now our Junior School Earth Angels team introduced two native stingless beehives to the campus as part of our long-term School Sustainability in Action Plan. As part of the budgeting and fundraising for this project, we sourced a number of books for the library on bees and beekeeping - ranging from non-fiction books aimed at professional beekeepers to picture books and non-fiction texts for the very young, and fiction stories for middle-grade readers where bees were either central characters or central to the plotline. Our aim was to provide resources which would not only further learning but also create a sense of story around our bees, spark curiosity and hopefully fire little imaginations as to what may be happening inside our hives and in the lives of individual bees. One such title was *How to Bee* by Bren MacDibble, which has been awarded a number of literary awards and is aimed at a reading audience of approximately 10 plus. *How to Bee* is set in future earth at a time when humans have so managed to pollute the world that bees have become almost extinct. Dystopian in nature, this book has been hugely popular at school and was our most popular read this year at my Year Six Girl Zone Book Club. MacDibble has cleverly woven issues of sustainability and nature into a gripping, often edge-of-your-seat storyline, and for those who have read it, bees will never be looked at in the same way again! One almost wants to bow down to the hives as you pass them on your way to the library – worker bees and queen bee alike!

There is incredible beauty in the quiet of a book, as there is in the relaxation of tending to gardens or just being in nature. Promoting a love of nature and an interest in sustainability in children is a critical element in building a society that respects and protects our world, and books which celebrate all these themes are crucial in starting and continuing the journey.

CHAPTER TWELVE

READING MINDFULLY

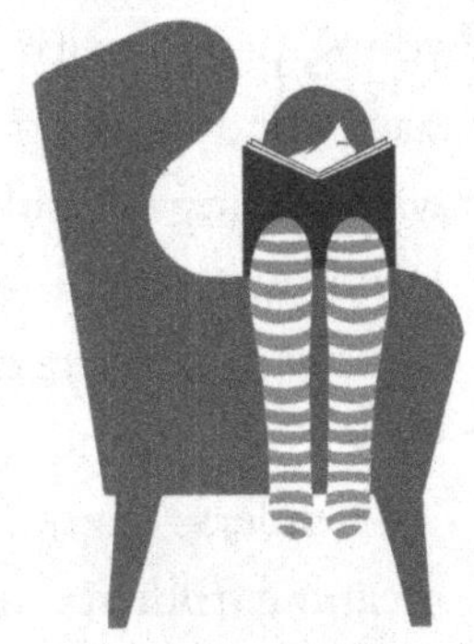

Mindfulness is something of a buzzword but it is one trend I am happy to support – there simply *has* to be an antidote to the fast-paced society which most of us find ourselves a part of today. At times it can feel like our lives are just spinning around and spluttering ahead, without the option to take a moment and just *be*; to focus our awareness on the here and now and calmly accept our thoughts and feelings as they come and go. I first heard about mindfulness from my father, who has been espousing the virtues of training your brain for as long as I can remember. What I find most interesting about Dad's passion for mindfulness is that his job is as a professor in policing, security and terrorism, specialising in violent extremism. For someone who spends much of his life researching a terribly negative aspect of the world, he's an exceptionally calm person, which I can only put down to how much energy he also puts into his mindfulness practice. So forget the buzzword and go with the ideas that underpin it.

For me, mindfulness is a way to improve my concentration and ability to be present. I know I am often in a state of mindfulness or 'flow' when I am engaged with and deeply 'inside' a beautiful book.

It provides a time of calm in an otherwise busy day. On a wider level, mindfulness has been shown to have a strong relationship to improved attentional functioning, including sustained, selective and executive attention, and the ability to improve working memory and brain function.[1] Mindfulness practices are used in the treatment of young people with attention difficulties and more recent studies have conducted research on the potential benefits with students with reading difficulties such as dyslexia.[2] It is logical that employing mindfulness techniques when reading would improve our ability to cope with sustained reading and reduce reading errors, as we are slowing down and following a straight path through a text.

Readers require sustained concentration to read and make meaning from literature. They need time to reflect and appreciate the nuances in language; we might call this deep reading, slow reading or mindful reading. Mindful reading is not skimming and scanning a text, highlighting and adding notes or reading while multitasking or becoming side-tracked by social media or your to-do list. Rather, reading mindfully requires the ability to be in the present moment, just you and the book, aware but without judgement of all that is occurring around you and inside you.

READING AS FLOW

Many keen readers may have experienced those times when they suddenly realise they have lost many hours in a good book having been in a state of 'flow'. Based on Dr Csikszentmihalyi's Flow Theory, flow is essentially characterised by a deep feeling of complete absorption in an activity. In a flow state, one is fully immersed in a feeling of complete focus, involvement and enjoyment in the process of performing an activity. We are not self-conscious or concerned by failure because there is complete oneness with the activity: the reader is with their book; the pianist is with their piano; the gardener is with the earth.

Georgina Manning, director of Wellbeing for Kids, is a mindfulness educator and I trained under her to become accredited as a Peaceful Kids facilitator. Her knowledge of the research behind mindfulness is extraordinary and she has unpacked some of the ideas around mindfulness and reading a little more here.

Georgina Manning

Ever read a page of a book and realised that you took in none of what you have just read? Your mind is filled with the day's ups and downs, and you end up going back and forth between past and present. Our minds are not focusing on the present and our body is on autopilot. We are there physically, with our eyes reading the text, but we are not processing the words, comprehending it or relating it to our lives. We can live each day on autopilot, going about our daily tasks, but not engaging our mind.

When we can bring our full awareness to what we are doing, we allow our minds to rest and be wholly attentive of the present moment and the joy this often brings. 'I can't wait to go on holidays and "get lost" in my book' is a phrase we often hear. It's interesting we wait until the holidays to allow ourselves to be lost in the moment, almost as though we need permission to stop and engage in a nurturing activity. In our fast-paced multitasking world, the process of getting lost in a book, reading, is almost seen as a luxury, only to be indulged in when everything else is done.

What takes us away from being mindful and allowing ourselves to be fully immersed in a good story? Is our fast-paced multitasking world so overwhelming to the mind that we have forgotten the art of just being? When we are in the 'being' as opposed to the 'doing' mode, we allow ourselves to be immersed in our present moment. If we are constantly up in our heads, going through our to-do lists, we are not allowing our minds to fully rest and rejuvenate.

Reading is one the easiest ways to practise entering the 'being' mode. Reading brings us into the present moment and takes us away from our to-do lists, and worries, which often activate our body's stress response. When we are engaged mindfully in a deeply relaxing and nourishing activity such as reading, this usually switches off our stress response and allows both our minds and our bodies to rest and have a calm awareness. As we experience that sense of calm by being present, we are training our brain to develop new neuropathways that help our brain to naturally become more mindful during our other day-to-day activities. The more we practise being mindful informally, the more we are naturally mindful at other times of the day.

Reading before we sleep has also become a lost art. The increase in screen time before bed is becoming an epidemic that is having catastrophic effects on the brain. As children's brains are growing, they particularly need time each day to rest and just play. They also need wind-down activities every night to help them to drift off into a deep, nourishing sleep. Going from screens straight to bed is extremely disruptive to children's sleep patterns and quality of sleep. If we don't allow our brains to slowly wind down from the day and immerse ourselves in a relaxing activity such as reading, we are still wired even in our sleep. Reading is one of the most powerful activities we can do for our brains before sleep. As an experiment, for two weeks try switching off all screens at least an hour before sleep, spend at least 30 minutes reading before bed and feel the benefits for yourself.

PRACTISE READING MINDFULLY

If you would like to practise reading mindfully, or encourage your children to, try the following: choose a time when you can focus on your reading for an extended period without distractions. Pick a book that engages you but will not exhaust you mentally. A print book will be a better choice than an ebook which comes with a suite of options and distractions, and the physicality of a print book can help you to focus. Pay attention to the book itself – the weight of it in your hands, the colour of the paper, the size of the font and how the font runs across the page. Read and stay present for as long as you can.

Like everything that is worth doing, mindfulness takes practice and I am certainly no expert nor do my current life circumstances allow for very much at all. But rather than worry that mindfulness is just one more thing to fit in, I continue to read about it and share books on mindfulness with my own children and the children in my school. I keep it in the front of my mind and in doing so I am aware it is there for me to fall back on when time and life circumstances shift and change, as they invariably do.

At school I am currently running a term-long mindfulness unit with students from kindergarten to Year Six. Library lessons focus on the art of reading mindfully and the skills one needs to develop to do this. We are looking at the research and science behind mindfulness and sharing beautiful picture books with mindfulness themes in each class. This is not something which sits outside of the realms of the school curriculum. Practising mindfulness can support the development of skills in self-management, self-awareness, social management and social awareness, which are four key ideas outlined in the Personal and Social Capability learning continuum in the Australian Curriculum.[3] Along with looking at the literature, each lesson ends with students spending quality time reading as mindfully as they can in the library, outside near our native stingless bees or perhaps under a tree in the playground. These lessons lay the groundwork for individual students and families to take onboard these concepts and practices. With the support of school management and classroom teachers, this unit is a structured and beneficial way to implement a whole-school approach to mindfulness.

BOOKS ENCOURAGING MINDFUL PRACTICES

The following books are suitable for introducing language and principles around mindfulness. They should start conversations with children about how they might be able to practise being mindful.

I Am Peace by Susan Verde, illustrated by Peter H. Reynolds (Abrams, 2017)

Take the Time by Maud Roegiers (American Psychological Association, 2010)

Making Mindful Magic by Lea McKnoulty (Tien Wah Press, 2015)

Sitting Still Like a Frog by Eline Snel (Shambhala Publications Inc, 2013)

Is Nothing Something? by Thich Nhat Hanh, illustrated by Jessica McClure (Parallax Press, 2014)

Silence by Lemniscates (American Psychological Association, 2012)

A Handful of Quiet by Thich Nhat Hanh (Parallax Press, 2012)

Slow Down World by Tai Snaith (Thames and Hudson, 2017)

A Quiet Girl by Peter Carnavas (University of Queensland Press, 2019)

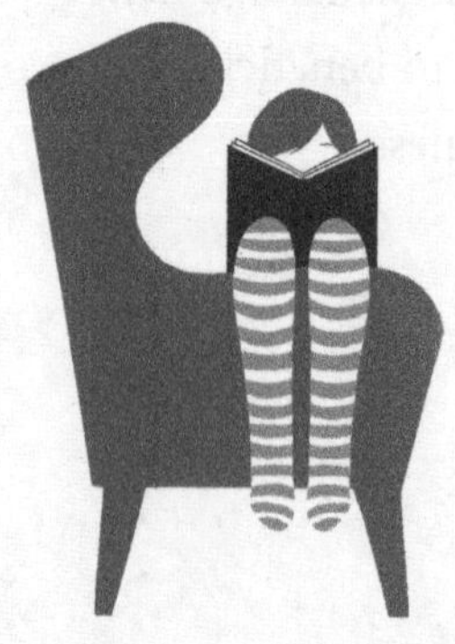

CHAPTER THIRTEEN

ACKNOWLEDGING AND REFLECTING DIVERSITY

Representing and reflecting diversity in literature is an important consideration for so many reasons, but there are two main ones and they dovetail perfectly into this book's broader themes. Children who read about lives different from their own develop more empathy for other individuals, and they will be inclined to read more if they can see themselves in stories. A number of movements have come into existence addressing discrimination and lack of diversity, and that aim to increase inclusivity. We Need Diverse Books is an organisation that advocates essential changes in the publishing industry to produce and promote literature that reflects the lives of all young people. These shifts in 'norms' have gained momentum in the last ten years or so and the #weneeddiversebooks movement has been central to this. There will never be enough books to cover all aspects of diversity because for every story that is told there is another, equally powerful story waiting in the slush pile.

Books featuring characters from diverse cultural backgrounds help young readers internalise multicultural sensibilities. Early reading experiences can and should play a role in sharing the joy of a rich variety of people and cultures around the world. It is pleasing to see more Asian, African and South American stories appearing among the European and American picture books that have dominated the market for so long.

Middle-grade readers are also being treated to a more diverse range of chapter books. Stories of refugees and immigrants are well represented in an age group that predominately leans towards humour and adventure. When we have a character who just happens to have a Chinese name, or who mentions that her parents travelled from Iran, or who is depicted as living in India, we are exposing our readers to situations they may never experience in their lifetime. Diversity in books creates a space for readers to accept other cultures without it being an 'issue'. Clever authors add details within the narrative that challenge readers without overtly 'telling'. An able-bodied person should be able to read about a character with a disability and recognise a human being, a real person they can empathise with. Carefully chosen books can form part of a powerful and subtle message of acceptance and connection and allow our young people to walk in the footsteps of others.

Diverse texts also play a crucial role in allowing readers to see their life reflected in story. Children from other countries, struggling with a new language and different customs, should be able to see faces similar to their own smiling out at them from the pages of a picture book. Young readers with disabilities need to see that their stories are worthy, that they are not alone. Older teens struggling with sexual orientation or experiencing racism or bullying long for books portraying them in positive ways. The importance of authenticity in representation is key. Allowing people of colour, mixed race, disability and varying sexual orientation to speak to an audience from a published position gives those voices credibility. Awareness of these issues is becoming more prominent and authors are becoming more conscious of the issues of sensitivity when writing about these subjects, particularly if they are not part of these groups being represented.

There is no excuse for taking on a story and then not doing everything possible to ensure that it is sensitively handled and compassionately told. We all have the freedom to write what we want, but we must also make sure we are making authentic decisions.

INDIGENOUS VOICES

I have known Des Crump and Michelle Witheyman-Crump for my entire teaching career. With more degrees than any one person should have, Des is a proud Gamilaroi man and an expert in Indigenous linguistics. Both he and Michelle have a keen interest in Indigenous children's literature.

Des Crump and Michelle Witheyman-Crump

Australian children's literature has embraced Aboriginal and Torres Strait Islander culture; though, one could argue that many of those stories reaffirm the idea of 'other' and 'different' rather than 'valid' and 'worthy'. Creation stories and depictions of remote community life have filled the literary landscape for years. Urban Indigenous voices are also becoming stronger and clearly recognised.[1]

The main reason for having Aboriginal and Torres Strait Islander books in schools and having non-Indigenous children reading them is that Australia has a shared history. Unfortunately, this history is more often told by non-Indigenous voices. It is now the time, not to mention proper and reasonable, that Aboriginal and Torres Strait Islander people are the storytellers of their own histories. Author and advocate Anita Heiss, and others, have raised awareness of the range of Aboriginal and Torres Strait Islander authors, and organisations such as BlackWords and the Indigenous Literacy Foundation have also played an important part in this process.[2]

Exposing young people to Aboriginal and Torres Strait Islander authors is not just about diversity, it is about providing authenticity to their world-view and allowing readers a glimpse of lives beyond their own. Aboriginal and Torres Strait Islander lives and stories are constantly changing and reflecting the world around them. Stories need to go beyond the stereotypes and historical moments that are stuck in time.

Storytelling is a personal process, particularly for Aboriginal and Torres Strait Islander writers whose lives and identity have been determined by a history of government policies and media stereotypes. Yarning Strong is a series that seeks to answer the question 'What's it like to be a young Aboriginal or Torres Strait Islander person in Australia today?' Stories written by Aboriginal and Torres Strait Islander authors unpack this question and provide the background content for teachers to bring it to life in the classroom.[3]

Respected author, academic and activist Tony Birch has also highlighted the critical need for non-Indigenous writers to create more authentic Indigenous characters, not 'stock' representations, advising authors to 'read, watch, look and listen to everything you can to engage with Indigenous issues'. Birch adds that experience with Aboriginal and Torres Strait Islander people and their daily lives can help create more rounded, nuanced Indigenous characters.[4] Author Gayle Kennedy, winner of the 2006 David Unaipon Award, and acclaimed author for children and adults Anita Heiss both reinforce the notion that Aboriginal and Torres Strait Islander literature should not be homogenised nor seen as a niche, but part of the rich literary diversity Australia has to offer.[5]

#OWNVOICES

The #ownvoices movement was created by the writer Corinne Duyvis and defines marginalised characters written by marginalised writers – so people of different racial backgrounds or minority groups being able to write about their circumstances, shifting the writing platform

BOOKS BY INDIGENOUS AUTHORS

My Australian Story: Our Race for Reconciliation by Anita Heiss (Omnibus Books, 2017)

Kookoo Kookaburra by Gregg Dreise (Magabala Books, 2015)

Nana's Land by Delphine Sarago-Kendrick (Magabala Books, 2004)

Home to Mother by Doris Pilkington Garimara (University of Queensland Press, 2006)

Follow the Rabbit-Proof Fence by Doris Pilkington Garimara (University of Queensland Press, 2006) (older readers)

Stolen Girl by Trina Saffioti, illustrated by Norma MacDonald (Magabala Books, 2011)

Black Cockatoo by Carl Merrison and Hakea Hustler (Magabala Books, 2018)

Deadly D & Justice Jones series by David Hartley and Scott Prince (Magabala Books)

Brontide by Sue McPherson (Magabala Books, 2018)

Mrs Whitlam by Bruce Pascoe (Magabala Books, 2016)

Sister Heart by Sally Morgan (Fremantle Press, 2015)

Remembering Lionsville by Bronwyn Bancroft (Allen & Unwin, 2016)

away from those with a predominantly Anglo-Saxon/Judeo-Christian background.

I first met Will Kostakis while he was being gushed over by a mob of senior school girls, all of whom had adored his novels like *The First Third* and *Loathing Lola* and wanted a selfie with him. With the release of his novel *The Sidekicks*, Will also began to tell his own story and came out to his legions of fans as gay. Here he shares with us why #ownvoices is a cause close to his heart.

Will Kostakis

When it comes to embracing diversity in literature – be it the author's identity and experiences, or those of the characters on the page – we are trending in the right direction. I say trending, when I really wish we were striding, leaping or ... already there.

We, perhaps without realising it, rank diverse identities in terms of acceptability. For instance, the same people who would insist I talk less about growing up gay when speaking to teens ('The focus should be on the text and the craft!') were the same people who, years or even minutes earlier, would ask me to reflect on my experiences growing up as a Greek-Australian. Both my sexuality and my heritage have shaped me as a person and, in turn, the texts I produce.

But one part of my identity is more palatable than the other.

A few years ago, I was invited to discuss my YA novel *The First Third* with a class of Year Ten girls who had recently finished a text study. As I entered the room, the teacher quietly cautioned me not to mention the gay character, Sticks. It was a request that took me by surprise, but I honoured it. I removed all mentions of one of the book's most prominent characters in my discussion of it. As a closeted gay man, the act of excising Sticks from my presentation was me diminishing the value of my own experiences to preserve my career.

At the talk's conclusion, I asked the students who their favourite character was, expecting them to name Yiayia, the character modelled after my own grandmother. Instead, one student named Sticks. I tried to steer the conversation back to unforbidden territory by asking their favourite scene. The same student raised her hand. She named the scene where Sticks explained losing his virginity to another boy. The girls around her nodded in agreement.

This fascinated me. I didn't comprehend why a group of – I assumed – heterosexual teen girls connected with a scene about a gay boy grappling with his sexuality. The answer shouldn't have been surprising.

'It helped me understand my friend Sam a little bit better.'

We talk about diversity in literature as if it only affects the people now seeing themselves on the page. I mean, it does, the impact is incredible. I remember the only gay content I encountered in high school English, William Shakespeare's Sonnet 20, feeling like a revelation to the Year Nine me, not because it reflected my own experience exactly, but because if Shakespeare could write about gay stuff, then maybe it was okay for me to live a life of … gay stuff. But reading that poem did not just allow the – it later turned out – three gay kids in that class to see themselves, it helped the twenty-odd other boys understand them a little bit better.

Diverse texts foster empathy. And young readers are curious. They crave that understanding of others. Whatever the misgivings of their gatekeepers, young readers will seek out the content that satisfies that curiosity. If they do not find it in their homes or libraries, they will search for it online.

Coming out as gay eight years into my career gave me an insight into the importance of supporting #ownvoices creators. The content of my work was mostly celebrated, particularly its diverse representations, but when I came out, my writing was viewed differently. We are, it seems, more comfortable with assumed-straight men writing gay characters than gay men writing them.

Straight Will was asked to speak at schools, and occasionally asked to steer clear of discussing gay characters. Gay Will's books were no longer appropriate for high school students. They were how-to manuals for deviant behaviour, political … They were the same books.

The professional costs for reflecting the world's diversity as a straight man were near zero, but reflecting that same diversity when I was more open about my identity became a high-wire act.

In a reading community where there are no consequences to coming out, sure, initiatives like #ownvoices might not be as important. Anyone can write anything so long as it is well-crafted, well-researched and well-intentioned. But that community does not exist, not yet anyway.

We're … trending towards it.

••

#OWNVOICES BOOKS

The Sidekicks by Will Kostakis (Penguin Books Australia, 2016) (older readers)

The Hate U Give by Angie Thomas (Balzer + Bray, 2017) (older readers)

Thai-riffic by Oliver Phommavanh (Puffin, 2010)

Does My Head Look Big in This? by Randa Abdel-Fattah (Pan Australia, 2005) (older readers)

We Are Okay by Nina LaCour (University of Queensland Press, 2019) (older readers)

George by Alex Gino (Scholastic US, 2015)

The Boat by Nam Le (Penguin Books Australia, 2009) (older readers)

Ida by Alison Evans (Echo Publishing, 2017) (older readers)

The Flywheel by Erin Gough (Hardie Grant Egmont, 2015) (older readers)

Inside Out and Back Again by Thanhha Lai (University of Queensland Press, 2012)

REFUGEES AND DISPLACED CHILDREN

With parents who were involved in supporting refugees since I can remember, I have been incredibly privileged to have spent my childhood running around with kids of different nationalities. I am still very dear friends with one particular family from Iran and Persian food featured in my top five cuisines as a child thanks to Pooran. I was aware of the adversity they had faced in coming to Australia and even as quite a young child I was well aware that a move such as this would not have been undertaken lightly. I had a deep sense that these were very brave people who must be showered with all the kindness our family and friends could offer them.

We are hopefully entering a time where our young people grow up with a far greater understanding of and empathy for refugees. While not every family will be directly involved with some of these families as I was, every child can develop their understanding of the issues facing refugees and displaced children through well-chosen literature. I have spoken at length throughout *Raising Readers* about how important books are in developing empathy and, when discussing diverse books, the concept of empathy comes into its own.

Many Australian children's and YA literature creators – both those who have entered Australia as refugees or immigrants and those born here – use the plight of refugees and displaced children to acknowledge and reflect diversity. Australian picture books and novels that give insight into these experiences are being read and acclaimed around the world. I have asked children's literature consultant Joy Lawn to discuss some of the very best titles about refugees to read and re-read with your own young people. I first met Joy when I became involved with the Children's Book Council of Australia Queensland branch. Her name is apt as this dear woman exudes joy and a sense of utter calm from her very being. In all her public lectures and her writing, Joy is articulate, insightful, considered and well researched. I remember the first time I heard her speak thinking, *One day I want to be just like her*. Joy tells me I cannot be like her because then I would not be me and what I offer in the world of children's literature is my own unique, accessible and amusing voice, which is different but just as valid. See? The woman is pure joy. She has a deep empathy for the plight of refugees and displaced children and her book recommendations below should be well noted.

Joy Lawn

I have learned that creators of children's and YA literature are often at the vanguard in addressing significant issues, which they explore with insight and empathy. Morris Gleitzman's *Boy Overboard*, John Marsden and Matt Ottley's *Home and Away* and Zana Fraillon's *The Bone Sparrow* have been formative in helping me vicariously 'live inside' a refugee experience and develop true compassion for those affected.

Teacup by Rebecca Young, illustrated by Matt Ottley, is a sublime rendering of the refugee situation. Its approach is oblique so that children are spared the horrors of what the boy who had to leave home and travel by boat to a new land may have experienced. He carried only a book, a bottle and a blanket, as well as a teacup with some earth from his home. When a seed sprouts in the teacup it becomes a symbol of food, protection, place and new life and the story becomes transcendent with hope. His journey is fraught but also full of wonder. The boy doesn't represent any particular race or culture. He is the universal displaced child.

In *Room on our Rock* by Kate and Jol Temple, illustrated by Terri Rose Baynton, a parent and child seal try to share a rock already occupied by a seal colony. Reading the story from front to back sends a message of exclusion, rejection and persecution. But reading from back to front shows acceptance, encouragement and hope. The rock is a transient shelter, small and crowded, but there is room for all.

In *Pea Pod Lullaby* by Glenda Millard, illustrated by Stephen Michael King, a mother, child, baby and dog are fleeing with a lantern in a boat – both iconic motifs in refugee stories. They help a polar bear, demonstrating their care for others despite their own peril. The illustrations are composed as wide horizontal panels, aptly representing the long journey, and the watercolour medium mirrors the ocean setting. The story is a lullaby, and the heightened, poetic words use the inclusive language of second person.

Idris is a child refugee born into a world of shadowed tents and fences in *Wisp* by Zana Fraillon, illustrated Grahame Baker Smith. When the wisp, a symbol of light and hope, flies in, only Idris notices it. He shares its memories with others, but when his own wisp finally arrives it brings a promise.

The Kingdom of the Lost series by Isobelle Carmody is a dystopian post-apocalyptic quest. The characters become displaced after they leave their home. The author knows that young people are concerned for the poor and homeless. She uses the fantastic as a mode to explore real-world issues. Even though Isobelle is a strong activist for refugees, she submerges the issues to honour the story. Refugees and slavery feature realistically and allegorically in this series.

Blossom by Tamsin Janu is subtle speculative fiction that may echo the experiences of those who are different. Lottie opens the door to a strange little girl with dark skin and hair. The girl is mute and holding a flower so Lottie names her Blossom. Lottie pretends they're sisters. When Blossom is found to be an alien with green blood and no heart, Lottie tries to protect her. 'Blossom' is a symbol of budding hope for the displaced.

The Blue Cat by Ursula Dubosarsky is a historical novel set around Sydney Harbour as World War II encroaches. The headmaster at Columba's school declares that Australia is a refuge for new boy Ellery, a Jew escaping the Holocaust. He is officially described as a 'Refugee Alien'.

In *Refuge* Jackie French subverts the realism genre into a ground-breaking alternate reality – an Australia dreamed by young refugees from different times and circumstances. The novel opens with Faris on a refugee boat to Australia. After his boat is swamped he plays a free-spirited ballgame with children from different countries and discovers that each has their own imagined Australia.

ADDITIONAL BOOKS ABOUT REFUGEES AND DISPLACED PEOPLE

Rainbow Bird by Czenya Cavouras (Wakefield Press, 2007)

Ali the Bold Heart by Jane Jolly, illustrated by Elise Hurst (Limelight Press, 2006)

Refugees by David Miller (Lothian, 2003)

Dancing the Boom Cha Cha Boogie by Narelle Oliver (Omnibus Books, 2005)

Hyram and B by Brian Caswell, illustrated by Matt Ottley (Hodder Children's Books Australia, 2003)

The Little Refugee by Anh Do and Suzanne Do, illustrated by Bruce Whatley (Allen & Unwin, 2011)

A True Person by Gabiann Marin, illustrated by Jacqui Grantford (New Frontier Publishing, 2007)

Ships in the Field by Susanne Gervay, illustrated by Anna Pignataro (Ford Street Publishing, 2012)

My Two Blankets by Irena Kobald, illustrated by Freya Blackwood (Hardie Grant Egmont, 2014)

My Name is Not Refugee by Kate Milner (The Bucket List, 2017)

Stepping Stones by Margriet Ruurs, artwork by Nizar Ali Badr (University of Queensland Press, 2017)

Zenobia by Morten Dürr, illustrated by Lars Horneman (University of Queensland Press, 2018)

CHAPTER FOURTEEN

READING THE DARK

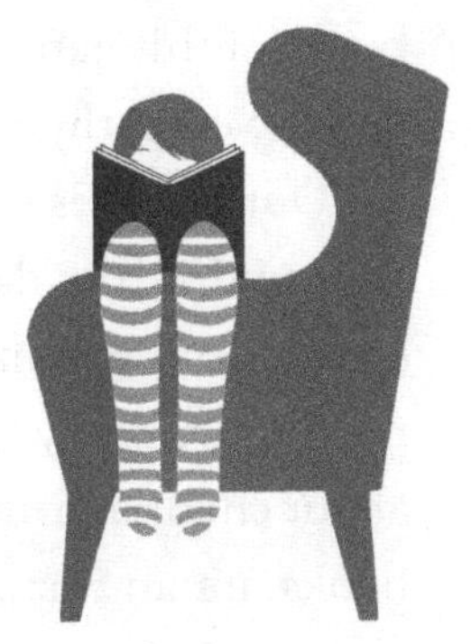

Those of you who read my blog will know that my family and I have experienced 'the dark' many times over. We have dealt with some really awful and quite scary health issues and we are intimately acquainted with grief. The death of my wild-spirited, huge-hearted little brother in 2012 shook our lives until we no longer knew which way was up and which way was down. In 2017, my beautiful and incredibly talented aunt passed away and then, mere weeks later, my husband Dan suffered a catastrophic heart attack in his sleep. Our children woke to the news that their beloved daddy had died and I had lost the other half of myself. My family and I are extremely close and we are fortunate that we have each other and a village of people who keep us afloat, but 'the dark' is still a journey that is mostly faced alone; no other person can ever comprehend the incredible minutiae of emotions that overwhelm your soul when you lose someone you love.

There are lots of young children in my extended family and they are well aware of the dark side of life. It is hard for us to not feel sad that their innocence has been taken from them, but it is impossible for it to be any other way. All we can do is to give them the tools to ensure they are resilient, empathetic and strong, and are able to deal with the twists and turns of life as best they can. Along with therapy and surrounding ourselves with our village, books dealing with grief and emotions have been very important to my family, and I believe books of this nature are important for *all* young people in helping to develop empathy, understanding, compassion and kindness.

Our house is still a happy place because there is always light to be found in the dark. It is full of laughter and shrieks of joy and screams of excitement over bodily function jokes, and we read the most ridiculously funny books. But we also read ones about feelings, about children living in poverty or war zones, and about grief. These books are an important part of our day-to-day reading. The light and the dark co-exist in life, as they do in literature, and we do our young people a disservice if we do not allow them to experience the full gamut of human emotions and experiences through carefully written, age-appropriate books.

The books I remember most from my childhood and early teens are *Charlotte's Web* (E. B. White), *Dicey's Song* (Cynthia Voigt), *When Hitler Stole Pink Rabbit* (Judith Kerr) and *Beginnings and Endings With Lifetimes in Between* (Bryan Mellonie and Robert Ingpen) and reading the blurbs of any of these books is enough to reduce me to tears. My mother provided me with stories that would make me cry myself to sleep at night. I can still remember the physicality of the feelings I experienced reading *So Much to Tell You* (John Marsden) and I desperately wanted to bring the main character, Marina, home with me for the weekend from her boarding school. At the time I had many school friends who were boarders and Marina leapt out of the pages and into my life. It was the first book I read many times over and even writing about it now makes me want to pull it out for another read, but I'm worried it won't reach the levels of greatness that it did in my early teens.

By Year Five, and especially Year Six and Seven, students ask library staff for 'books which will make me cry'. Just the other day, a new student in Year Six quietly asked me if I could show her where the section for sad books was in the library. After explaining that no such section existed, I pointed her towards my personal favourites – stories of bravery in the face of adversity and tales of families who survive despite the odds. From about the age of nine or ten, young people want to explore complex emotions and become more socially aware, and books are the perfect safe place to do this. A well-crafted story can transport the young reader into a situation they may never face in real life and soften and shape their thoughts around issues of humanity, justice and the world in which we live.

And yet, many parents would prefer their children continue to only read tales of wonder, magic and joy; that the books their children read reflect only the light in life. I completely understand and I'd love if it could be this way, but quality literature explores a range of experiences. I've had many long, sometimes tricky conversations with parents about books which explore dark themes. I've had complaints and concerns about books that deal with war, mental health, death and illnesses such as HIV and cancer. Many of these books are aimed at quite young children and their parents would very much prefer their innocence be preserved. I often ask them if they read *Charlotte's Web* as a child and commonly discover that it was one of their favourite books. Generally the penny drops and there is an 'ah-ha' moment as they remember that Charlotte's inevitable death was made bearable by the way her friends honoured her life and carried on with strength. I've had plenty of book stand-offs with parents, for many reasons, and I'm always (sometimes) happy to agree to disagree, because at the end of the day it is the parent's right to decide what is appropriate for their child. However, I talk with them about how it's our job as parents to protect our children from hurts and heartache, but also to develop in them the resilience which will carry them through tough times. I don't know of a better and more gentle way to introduce young people to 'the dark' of life than through age-appropriate, carefully chosen literature while they sit on the lap of a loved adult.

Author Shona Innes is a psychologist working with children and her Big Hug Books series for an early childhood to primary school audience deals with issues such as grief, bullying, family breakdown, body image and online safety. The language in each of the books is spot on and the stories are engaging and appealing to young children. I highly recommend them for every home, school and library collection. Shona shares with us her thoughts on how literature can support young people through the dark times in their life.

Shona Innes

To help a young person through dark times, indeed to help anyone of any age, we need to understand how the problem is for them. What are their experiences? What did they notice? What did they think about?

For the very young, concepts such as thoughts and feelings can be too big for them to understand. As we develop, our brain learns first to deal with the physical, touchable things around us. Only later in development are we able to notice we have thoughts ... and then, later still, we can have thoughts about our thoughts. The very young can express their feelings, but not stand back from their feelings to regulate them. Young children are usually much more in the moment. They can remember things from their past, but they may not be able to articulate those things in words nor understand their relevance to how they are feeling and behaving.

To make sense of the world, young children need more tangible and touchable objects to manoeuvre and manipulate. Stories with pictures (sometimes with additional puppets, toys, or that thing we just made with boxes and glue) can provide the link between something that happens in the story and a child's own experiences. We can use a picture book to talk about things that are difficult to talk about, and illustrations can help us emphasise emotions and encourage perspective taking. We can also see through a picture book the impact that a character's actions have on other characters. Indeed, the very process of reading together is an intimate activity that usually requires some closeness and undivided attention – safety and attention are two other necessary components of any healing process.

Sharing a book with a child can simply be the start of an important conversation. However, sometimes parents and teachers – because of their own experiences and emotions – can be reluctant to talk about dark topics with children. It is natural that adults want to protect children and I know that some worry that, if they talk to a child who is having a difficult time or needs to know some 'dark' news, they could make things worse instead of making it better.

There's another important concept that psychologists consider when they work with children and that is a process called 'generalisation'. When you give a child some new ideas or ways to manage their troubles they may think about them as things they do just when they are with the psychologist or in the psychologist's room or only with the particular problem you talked about that day. Children can need some help to generalise – to move the ideas from the room or place or time where they've talked about them and take them to use in other places like the playground, bedtime or school. We can help them generalise by practising in different locations and different situations, but we can also help generalisation by sharing the concepts used in sessions with other important adults in a child's life. The other adults can then prompt children to use new skills in other places.

It's a very exciting time to be a psychologist helping young people. We now know more than ever before about how children's brains change as they grow. This new information helps us to make sense of so many things we notice as a child moves from infancy through early childhood, the teen years, young adulthood and then into adulthood.

We now know that it is quite 'normal' for teens to experience more strongly felt emotions. Teens can become very interested in dark things and the troubles and dramas of others. They begin to have the capacity to relate and process darker themes. Changes to their developing brains can sometimes lead to differences in how emotions feel and they can go looking for bigger doses of things in order to experience pleasure – louder music, faster cars and juicier gossip. We think this might have something to do with the primal desire to push boundaries and explore new lands so that our gene pool has a healthier, more diverse mix. So, it is unsurprising that teens desire more emotion and excitement in their books. Not surprisingly, a teen brain wants more from a 'good read' and they can use books to escape and explore emotions and ideas without leaving the comfort of home.

Books can be useful in psychological interventions with children as a way of sharing experiences about dark times, discussing feelings, and reflecting on options. They can open pathways to further conversations and provide connection. In the same way you might keep a first aid kit for minor medical emergencies, having some books about darker issues can serve as your emotional first aid kit – not a substitute for a professional consultation, but a good way to get conversation rolling to see if more help is necessary.

....

My own experience reading emotionally complex books to all the children in my professional and family life has led me to believe, quite passionately, that children are more able to deal with the light and the dark of life than we give them credit for. The very best creators of children's books weave sorrow and heartbreak with love and comfort. These books develop empathy and resilience in our children. But books are also an escape – so don't fall into the trap of handing 'books about grief' to a grieving child without also including some humour or fantastical ones. The 'dark' books should be available to, but not forced upon, a child. The truth is that the world is full of love and of devastation. Good writers help their readers to see that the darker shades of this world can be made bearable by offering hope and showing that there is always light, even just a pinprick of it, in the dark. And, of course, my hope is that every child has someone in their life who loves them and will read to them.

CHAPTER FIFTEEN
HOW-TO GUIDES

HOW TO BE AN EXCELLENT BOOK GIFTER

We always give books as gifts for christenings, housewarmings, weddings, kids' parties, new babies, or for any occasion, really. It's become a bit of a joke as we hand over the gift-wrapped book-shaped package. I know that a book is the last thing a three-year-old is going to be excited about at their party, but the parents are usually happy, and the child will be happy later, just not at the party when all they want is shiny new toys.

It's important to choose book gifts with care as the right book will be treasured for many years, even through generations. I have several from my childhood gifted to me by family friends and inscribed that I still hold very dear and will never give away.

We've had many friends comment over the years that they love reading the books we've given to their children. Just the other day a friend sent a message saying they were unpacking a shelf at their new house and noticed that all the books their three children had chosen to keep were from us – I gave myself a mental high five. I often choose books that will appeal to our adult friends as much as to their child: for builder friends I've chosen books with hammers and cubbyhouses; for friends who we spent our youth with at music festivals I gift books written by favourite songwriters; foodie friends get kids' cookbooks or food-focused picture books; and our dentist (and the girls' aunt) often receives books about the tooth fairy or teeth. You wouldn't believe how many books about teeth there are, though I've not yet been game to gift her *Demon Dentist* by David Walliams just in case she takes offence. No one wants an upset dentist wielding a drill!

The following are some tips when you are ready for some serious book gifting:

- It is tempting to grab books from the bargain bin, but I urge you to walk past those, unless you see something you know is fabulous and shouldn't be in there to start with. Quality books often cost more, but I can assure you they will be treasured. Work out what you'd spend on a toy for a child and buy one or two beautiful books with that money instead.
- When you find the perfect book gift for an occasion such as a christening or birthday ... buy it in bulk. The year PudStar turned eight I found the perfect set of three books for all parties she attended that year so I purchased ten sets on sale. One of the few times I was organised with presents and, by golly, it felt good! Similarly, I have a particular title that I like to gift for the birth of a first child, *Puffling* by Margaret Wild and Julie Vivas. It's a good one for reducing emotional parents to tears and is a total keepsake.
- If you or your child would like to gift something with the book, try and find something in theme. My tween now insists on this because 'I'm so embarrassed that you always give books and so embarrassed that you're a librarian and so embarrassed by ...' She is embarrassed by me in general. We've done lots of packs for five-

year-old parties of kids' gardening gloves, glass containers and watering cans with my favourite book on growing terrariums, *Tiny World Terrariums* by Michelle Inciarrano and Katy Maslow. For tweens, a particularly good title about hairstyles like *Hair Romance* by Christina Butcher goes well with one of those ridiculously oversized and overpriced hair bows or clips and ribbons.

- Inscribe the books you gift, either with a message that relates to the book and why you gave it to them and/or a personal message. The books I've kept from my own childhood are the ones that are inscribed to me. It's so lovely to see the dates and remember who gave them to us. I also have all my old Miffy books and each has my name written by Mum, with the year it was purchased – such a librarian! Mum still writes in all the books she gives to her grandchildren and they really enjoy 'finding' a book that she has inscribed on their shelves. The first gift that was given to me when I had PudStar was the beautiful book previously mentioned, *Puffling*, and I cried. The inscription reads: *One day you'll be big enough, tall enough, strong enough and brave enough to leave your nest and take on the world. But until then your lovely mum and your proud dad will be there for you and will cherish you. We'll be watching. Welcome to the World. The Buckleys.* Okay, I had just had a baby, hadn't slept for about three days and the baby wouldn't stop crying, but I still tear up every time I read this inscription.
- Keep a list. I keep lists in a little notebook of all the books I've given to family members and the children of family friends and some of these lists have been going for ten or so years now. It's super handy to look back so I don't double up on titles.
- Don't go for the obvious. I would rarely gift a classic book or super popular book to a child as they will very likely have it already. Things like *The Very Hungry Caterpillar* and *Guess How*

Much I Love You are obvious choices for newborns so I steer well clear of them and go for something just as heartfelt but lesser known.

- Own the 'book aunty/uncle/friend' title with pride. My sister gives money to all the nieces and nephews and the children look forward to this tradition. I'm the book aunt!

HOW TO PLAY WITH SIGHT WORDS

There are many people who have come up with amazing sight word games and a quick search of Pinterest will have you either swooning or gagging at the insane number of ideas to support your child in learning the 'Magic 100' sight words. I applaud those of you who spend hours cutting up and writing on paint sample cards to create innovative and aesthetically pleasing sight word games. Sadly, I am not one of those people, although I do have a few favourite strategies for learning sight words, which are listed below. I've tried to cover my bases with learning styles and to incorporate some physical movement because wriggly little people learn sight words on the go beautifully.

Sight word splat

Draw a series of flies on white paper with a thick black pen. Photocopy these twenty to thirty times, laminate and cut out individual flies. With a whiteboard marker, write sight words for the week on the flies and place them and one or two fly swats (preferably never used to splat *actual* flies) in an accessible location in the house (ours either go on the coffee table or are tacked onto the fridge).

You can play sight word splat a number of ways:

- One-person game: adult or older sibling calls out a sight word and child 'splats' the appropriate word fly.

- Two-person game: adult or older sibling calls out a word and whoever splats the word fly first, collets that fly. Child with the most dead flies wins.
- Independent: encourage (or bribe) your child to pick up their fly swat every morning before breakfast and 'splat and say' each of the words on the flies.

Sight word hop

Write sight words in chalk on pavers in the yard. Have your child hop onto each word and say it as they land on it. You can go hopscotch or stepping stone style.

Sight word parking lot

On a sheet of paper draw a shopping centre 'parking lot' and write one sight word in each parking bay. Have your child 'park' their toy car on the sight words you call out. I used to leave this one set up outside ChickPea's Sylvanian Family nursery, and as she dropped her babies off to kindy in her games, I often heard her parking on a particular word. Honestly, incidental learning is the best and requires no effort on your part so it is a win all round.

Sight word craft sticks puzzles

For this you will need coloured craft sticks (like paddle-pop sticks but in colours) and a permanent marker. Hold two craft sticks of the same colour together side by side and write a sight word over the two sticks. Each sight word should go on different coloured stick for an easier version, or jumble the colours up if you want to take the difficulty up a level. Separate and mix up your puzzle sticks and then have your child match the words up.

Sight word playdough

Now that I've convinced you all that I'm über mum re: sight word learning, let me tell you that I love making playdough. Playdough is the simplest thing in the world to make and, unlike other complicated activities you may set up, playdough does actually entertain children (and adults) for a long time. These days people get really fancy and add essentials oils, glitter and sometimes dried flower petals to their mix. Playdough is brilliant for fine motor skill development (crucial for holding a pencil) and it can be used for so many learning games. I use it in a few ways:

- I have a set of small letter cookie cutters, which PudStar often used to cut letters out of playdough for ChickPea and to construct her sight words. Or you can just roll out the dough and use the cutters to 'stamp' the words into the dough.
- Letter beads can be stuck into playdough, along with other small plastic toys – fun to create sentences, for example, 'the' in letter beads plus a plastic dog equals 'the dog'.
- Roll out snakes and make the letters of sight words.
- Use a skewer to write sight words in the dough.

Sight word highlighters

This is so obvious that I shouldn't even write it here but, dear glory, I love this one. Rip out a page of an old book (I'm a librarian – I have a lot of damaged, culled books to go through) or use a page of a magazine or newspaper. Give your child a highlighter and get them to scan through the text and highlight any sight words they can find.

Sight word spotto

We play spotto with yellow cars when we are driving. I don't know who even started it. But I also used to do sight word spotto. Five sight words are stuck on the back of the passenger seat for the kids to see. They simply scan signs as you drive and yell out 'spotto' and the sight word when they see one. This usually ends in screaming and tears but all for a good cause.

HOW TO HOST A BOOK PARTY

I'm a fan of book-themed parties. Aside from the obvious joy of seeing a book come to life, the theming is all done for you thanks to the text and illustrations. Let me take you through the process of creating your very own book-themed party at home, keeping in mind that I am a librarian, not a party planner, and I have no thoughts of a career change anytime soon!

- Select your child's favourite picture book or book series or decide what sort of book party you want and subtly convince your child that it's the best book ever.
- Read the book a number of times and pick out some quotes you could use and some theme ideas based on the illustrations and/or the text. Write a list of any food mentioned in the book and brainstorm what sort of food would go well with the book.
- Decide on a colour theme or over-arching theme and stick with it; don't try to cram every element of the book into a party. Keep it simple, streamlined and cohesive.
- Search online for any teaching notes or worksheets that accompany the book. You'll be surprised how many of your favourite children's books have ready-made ideas for activities and party games. You may even find publisher-produced, copyright-free for personal use images you can use for cupcake toppers, invites and party bags.
- Create invitations for the party using either the cover of the book or any images found on the publisher's website. Issues with copyright will come about if you commercialise your party

or share images of it online, but for a home party the use of the cover to promote the party to friends and family will not cause issues. Similarly, using images found on publisher websites is generally fine if they are for personal use.

- Start the party with a reading of the book and explanation of the themed food and party games.
- Party favours may be a copy of the book, if you can find them at a reasonable price, or copies of any other books which you can source at a low cost. My own children have become quite used to the fact that our party bags are always books. Sometimes I add a lollipop to placate them!

We've hosted many book parties at home and in local parks, and two of my favourites are outlined in a little more detail below, as well as a few others which friends have hosted and are featured on my blog. All of these relate to specific titles but could be adapted to suit other books with similar themes.

Where the Wild Things Are party

This theme was perfect for ChickPea's second birthday party because we used to talk about ChickPea being a 'wild thing'. Poor ChickPea had terrible reflux as a baby and it wasn't her fault but she did rather yell and roar.

The food and décor for this one was super easy as there is a huge amount of *Where the Wild Things Are* paraphernalia out there. I found printable cupcake toppers to purchase online, posters and bunting and then went with mustard-yellow as the theme colour. Food was all monster- or jungle-related: chocolate cupcakes with chocolate rocks, chocolate grass and cupcake toppers; chocolate spoons with green and mustard-coloured sprinkles; homemade sherbet cones filled with green sherbet and green and mustard sprinkles; and a selection of savoury food such as monkey-shaped sandwiches and quiches with jungle palm toppers. The cake was a huge wild chocolate creature with lots of chocolate rocks and jungle leaves.

Activity-wise we did some monster stomping dancing and statues, pin the tail on the monster, dress-ups for all (lots of monster masks and wigs), and a treasure hunt. *Where the Wild Things Are* badges, stickers and tattoos plus a gift edition copy of the actual book made up the party favours for this great family celebration.

Stomping dinosaur party

At three, ChickPea was still cranky, wild and now stomping, and had developed a dinosaur obsession. Her favourite book at the time was one my mother gave her about a little boy who accidentally grows dinosaurs in his garden. It is a very long picture book and ChickPea wanted it every night for over a year! Even now at seven she goes back to this one regularly.

We went with a purple, green and yellow theme for this party as these were the predominant colours in the book, and who doesn't love clashing colours? Partygoers dug for dinosaur fossils in sand, made little dinosaur gardens to take home (in small terracotta pots with succulents and a plastic dinosaur), collaged dinosaurs, painted mud dinosaurs (from another favourite dinosaur book) and danced to dinosaur stomp songs. Food was sandwiches cut with a dinosaur cookie cutter, dinosaur fossil biscuits, cupcake liners filled with fruit and topped with dinosaur toppers, dino egg scones, cake pops covered in chocolate sand, dinosaur-topped cupcakes and a volcano and dinosaur cake. Party favours were bags with flowers seeds to 'grow your own dinosaurs' as in the book.

Other book parties we have held and which make great general party themes include:

A samurai versus ninja party based on the Samurai vs Ninja series by Nick Falk and Tony Flowers

Thelma the Unicorn party

Alice in Wonderland party

The Fairy Dancers party based on the book by Natalie Jane Prior and Cheryl Orsini

Bollywood party based on several books set in India and one which was Bollywood themed

Flower Fairies party based on the books by Cicely Mary Barker

Spy party based on the Truly Tan books by Jen Storer

Disco party based on several disco-themed books

Miffy party based on the books by Dick Bruno

Pearlie in the Park party based on the series by Wendy Harmer

Little Blue and Willow tea set party based on the picture book by Gaye Chapman

HOW TO CREATE A LIBRARY MAKERSPACE

If the idea of a makerspace in your library or school appeals, the next thing to think about is how to bring this idea to life so that the community has access to a safe and creative space for exploration. It's vital to know your students' interests and passions as you resource your space. Supportive school leadership teams are key in introducing makerspaces to the school library environment so advocacy is the first step before launching into setting one up. This section is a case of do as we say not as we do, as I have learnt a thing or five hundred along the way, and my mistakes and learnings will save you some time – and spare you some squealing in the library after the hot glue gun makes contact with skin.

The space

You may be in the privileged position to have a purpose-built space or be in the throes of designing such a space. What's more likely is that you will need to transform an existing area in your library into a makerspace. We claimed a classroom space in our library and reinvented it as our makerspace zone, lining the walls with shelves and boxes of neatly labelled equipment (library staff are clearly the ones to take on this task as we love creating order). Our idea was that the walls would be lined with equipment and the central area would be a space where students could work on the ground or at movable tables, depending on the project. It is vital that any space for creating can be left 'as is' over days and even weeks as creation takes time, projects need to be refined, and cleaners and people like me who like to bin things need to hold back and allow projects in development to remain in place on the floor or shelves.

The materials

Many makerspace activities you will see online are high tech options: electric circuits, squishy dough, conductive paint, coding, robotics and 3D printers. Not all learning opportunities in a makerspace environment need be high tech; in fact, some of the very best of learning experiences are created with cardboard, masking tape and items found in your school skip bin or during the kerbside collection. Clean recycled materials abound in our library and as an added bonus we are incorporating some strong messages about the value of recycling. Our makerspace started with low tech materials and ideas. Over time we have incorporated and acquired more advanced technology as funding has allowed.

Low tech (available to children at all times): scrap cardboard, cardboard rolls, boxes, cardboard saws, cardboard screws and hooks, masking tape, duct tape, Washi tape, scissors, glue, paper clips, hook and loop

Velcro, fabric scraps, wool, wire, foam, paper cups, plastic bottles, balloons, paddle-pop sticks, aluminium foil, straws, ping-pong balls, paint, playdough, needles and thread, string, wool, rubber bands.

LEGO is a great resource in a makerspace as it allows students to design and build and is endlessly versatile. LEGO walls, tables and corners are an invitation for children to create. Other construction equipment such as blocks, melting beads, electric blocks and other commercial construction materials that allow free play and exploration are also great.

Medium tech (used with adult supervision and otherwise kept out of reach of children): copper tape, electric paint, foil, selection of batteries, conductive threads, LEDs, wire, DC hobby motors, vibration motors, conductive and non-conductive dough, alligator clips, hot glue gun, balsa wood pliers, hammers, nails, screwdrivers, screws, split pins, bull dog clips, metal press studs, NeoPixels, LilyPad switches, Gemma boards.

High tech (used with adult supervision where needed and if budget allows you to dream!): iPads, computers, tablets, visualisers, recordable microphones, drones, droids and robots, 3D printers, 3D doodle pens, XY plotter with laser engraver, soldering iron, iron, sewing machine, computer building kits (Piper), electric snap circuits, Makey Makey kits, littleBits, Arduino, circuit stickers (Chibitronics), green screen, laser cutter, VR goggles.

The existing library resources

Many of our students have been inspired with makerspace projects after delving deep into our extensive non-fiction collection. Very early on in our makerspace journey we made a point of using what we had and what we know and this has paid dividends in terms of students also gaining a far greater insight into the workings of the

Dewey decimal system and the value of knowing your way around a library.

We created shelf markers and took students on 'tours' of the non-fiction collection to unearth where all the 'making' gems might be. These are now some of the most popular sections of our non-fiction collection: craft, sewing, construction, gardening, engineering, robotics, computers.

In terms of our fiction collection, virtually every single one of our early makerspace ideas was sparked by a picture book or CBCA-shortlisted book. Our first CBCA Book Week after we started our makerspace, we held an incredibly successful maker fair. We created items found in stories, made marble runs which took us through the narrative of a story as the marble rolled to each point, and created cardboard worlds based on the settings of stories.

We used picture books which highlighted the value of tinkering and 'having a go' to introduce makerspace language and ideas to the students. Quotes from books related to making were written over the windows and added to quote cards and signage around the library. Books were, and always will be, at the centre of our library makerspace.

The technology

The library is the place where technology is housed and the space where technology can lead the way in discovering and learning. Through her interest in enhancing student learning, my teaching partner Jackie is constantly on the look-out for technology that engages young people. For example, during library lessons, students were guided in exploring and playing with iPad apps to create animations or tell stories or biographies with augmented reality. Virtual reality and augmented reality technology allowed our students to create, experience and learn in virtual worlds.

The community

Connecting with 'makers' in the school community is the very best way to begin. Put a call-out in the school newsletter and there will be countless volunteers to teach knitting, crafting, engineering, electronics, gardening, woodwork and painting. They will be giving the gift of not just their knowledge but also enthusiasm. Makerspaces help to build community within a school or library environment and undoubtedly increase the learning opportunities, skills and knowledge of students.

The funding

School budgets may be getting tighter and tighter but where there's a will, there's a way. Many schools have used grant money, as grants of between $2000 and $5000 are often awarded to organisations to cover the costs of things such as equipment, software, and consumables needed to establish makerspaces. The government recognises the need for more students to participate in science, technology, engineering and mathematics (STEM) so is offering grants to schools and institutions to facilitate this. Money from the school parents and friends association or fundraising community events can be used to fund the technology, tools and materials in their makerspaces.

HOW TO CREATE A BOOK WEEK COSTUME

I am a Book Week tragic from way back. I have vivid childhood memories of planning my Book Week costumes with my mum. I know some people dread the planning of the Book Week costumes so hopefully this how-to will take away some of the pain and swap it with some fun.

There are a wealth of ideas online for book character dress-ups so there is no need for me to re-create such a list here. Instead I'm adding some ideas into the mix for creating meaningful costumes that can help bring the book to life and allow your child to really step into the shoes of their favourite character.

I always let my children choose their own Book Week characters – within reason – I'm not doing a dragon costume anytime soon! On the whole I find that most children choose characters who look a little like them because they connect with books which reflect their own life. Their costume may then be as simple as them wearing casual clothes in the style of their favourite character and deciding on a motif or element from the book to add to their outfit. One year PudStar went as Pippa from Belinda Murrell's *Pippa's Island: The Beach Shack Cafe* and wore shorts and a T-shirt. The book is set on a tropical island and has lots of talk of cupcakes so we added skewers with images of pineapples and cupcakes and a thumbnail of the book cover to her hair bun along with a stack of fake tropical flowers. When these skewers were poked into her hair (those bun doughnut things are like florist foam, I've discovered!), she was instantly transformed into Pippa. Adding those little extra elements that reflect the book is what takes a costume from 'pulled this out of my drawer this morning' to innovative and an expression of the child's love for a book or character.

If the costume doesn't make it obvious who the book character is, I always encourage my children and students to either carry the book with them or make a book cover lanyard to wear around their neck to identify which book they are from. Such a simple addition to a costume but it really does allow everyone to get into the spirit and, as an added bonus, seeing all those book covers around the schoolyard is perfect advertising for what you should read next.

If possible, allow plenty of time to prepare a Book Week costume – perhaps do as I say, not as I do. Lately my costumes are a bit 'on the fly', but in previous years I have taken note through the year of favourite books in our house and start talking about 'who we'll be' months before Book Week. In über-organised years I've set up the chosen book on a shelf and we'll talk about the character and what clothing items best represent them and add elements from home. Anything we need to buy to add to the costume we can then source in plenty of time.

Use what you have at home. From a young age my children have adored dress-ups and I've added to their box over the years so that we now have quite the collection. This comes in handy for Book Week each year, but costumes aren't the only thing you can use. I love seeing netball and soccer uniforms on show and one year I had about eight girls all come in netball uniform as characters from the Netball Gems series. This actually led to a borrowing spree of these books, which is entirely the outcome we librarians want from the Book Week dress-up day! We don't organise the Book Week parade to torture parents, caregivers and teachers - we actually use it as promotion and celebration of books!

Simple is good. Some of the cutest costumes I see are so simple and every year I think, *I must remember that idea for next year*. Last year a girl came as the cutest little cat from *Mrs Mancini* - she wore all black and had a cat ear headband with a nose and whiskers drawn on her face. She was carrying her *Mrs Mancini* book proudly throughout the parade and was completely in character. Another lovely one was a child dressed up as *Audrey of the Outback*, wearing plain clothes but carrying a billycan with a photocopy of the cover stuck to the outside.

Educator costumes

I talk all the time about reading role models, and Book Week is one of those times in the school year where I hope that all teachers, support staff, grounds staff and classroom volunteers try to up the reading ante: to bring books to life and celebrate them and demonstrate that you believe in the power of words and reading. Dressing up for

Book Week shows students that you care about books and you have favourite characters, too. It can be as easy or as complex as you like, but I urge all school staff to make the effort.

When I was a young classroom teacher, I would spend months planning my Book Week costumes and they became more and more elaborate each year. As the full weight of just what it meant to be a teacher became clear, the days of going to 90s raves and music festivals in all my glitter/tulle/coloured-hair glory disappeared and instead I channelled my love of OTT outfits into my Book Week costumes. Early in my career I went as the White Witch from Narnia and my costume consisted of a very large white ballgown, a very tall crown which had to be pinned to my head and a lot of silver glitter over my face, neck and arms. I had a rather long drive to school and my car decided that this was the day it would break down, on the side of a busy highway at peak hour. I have never really recovered from this.

Now slightly worn down by life and of an age where too much glitter isn't going to work for me, I've toned down my costumes accordingly. But I still love a good Book Week outfit and there are plenty of simple options for teachers. Albus Dumbledore, Filius Flitwick or one of the other Hogwarts professors from the Harry Potter series are popular choices each year. A Mary Poppins costume can be as easy as a fitted white shirt, red bow tie, black skirt and an umbrella; although one year a science staff member made herself the most gorgeous Mary Poppins outfit and I'm certain it inspired some children to hunt down a copy of this book from the library. If you're looking for a group costume, the crayons from *The Day the Crayons Quit* by Drew Daywalt and Oliver Jeffers is a great choice, especially for early childhood educators. I also love seeing schools of teachers dressed as Rainbow Fish (Marcus Pfister). Another fun idea is to be playful with your role at the school - for example, one year all the music department staff came as the musicians from *The*

Flying Orchestra by Clare McFadden. Another highlight was when our principal came as Enid Blyton's beloved character Elizabeth Allen from *The Naughtiest Girl in the School* – the students thought it was hilarious!

HOW TO RUN A READERS' COMPETITION

For anyone who would like to set up a readers' competition or become more involved in an existing one, I highly recommend a Readers' Cup or Story Sport-style competition.

The books

Organise multiple copies of the books to be used in the competition considering a range of genres, subject matter and reading abilities. Ensure a mix of male and female characters and authors. Often books you have used for set novels in the past and have multiple copies of are useful for a Readers' Cup competition, as are sets of novels purchased as classroom readers. You will need to ensure you can either borrow copies from local schools or public libraries in your area or that the book is in print and easily accessible for families.

Introducing the competition to students

- Arrange class visits or promote the competition during library borrowing times or lunchtimes or whatever has been decided upon.
- Prepare posters (online or paper versions) listing the books to be read, the rules and the dates and times of all heats.
- Select sections to read from some of the books and promote the titles.
- Collect entry forms for teams of four.

Preparing the competition

- Write enough questions for each book (usually four to six per book). Prepare extra questions to cater for the possibility of a tie in the final. Share the reading load with other teachers/teacher librarians. Questions are knowledge-based rather than asking students to philosophise over a particular title.
- We prep approximately thirty general literature questions for audience/parent participation between each student round.
- For several years we have also prepared a 'creative challenge' to include some making in the competition and ensure that all types of learners are catered for. These have included designing a new cover for a book and presenting teams with a 'mystery bag' of materials to design and make something significant from one of the books.
- Prepare a timetable for the heats and the final and publicise this to staff and students.
- We have been using an online quiz tool, Kahoot!, for the past few years in order to blend some technology into our competition. All questions are entered into Kahoot! before the event so that students work in team mode to answer questions about the books. This allows us to use visuals or videos uploaded into the program and adds a different element.
- Organise prizes (decide early on how they will be paid for):
    - First prize – cup/medal for each team member (plus, if funds permit, book voucher/book)
    - Second prize – book voucher/book
    - Third prize – book voucher/book
    - Prizes for participation in the heats – lollies/bookmarks

The format of the competition

- Participants read the selected books in advance.
- Teams of four are usually seated at tables, and may have decorated their table with their team name and/or mascot. They may or may not have a team uniform or costume.
- There is one round of questions for each book which are asked by an MC (teacher, teacher librarian or guest author).
- After each question is asked by the MC, students are given thirty seconds to one minute to confer as a group and complete their written answer.
- Answers are usually collected at the end of each round and a group of scorers mark them with points given for correct answers, usually two points for a correct answer and part points for an incomplete answer. The MC may give progressive scores which helps to increase the hysteria, fun, competition and noise factor.
- The team with the highest score win trophies and books and advances to the next level of the competition, after much cheering and happy crying and screaming!

HOW TO START A BOOK CLUB

Book clubs for children can help with confidence and public speaking and encourage them to read for both pleasure and study. It also affords children the opportunity to discuss and recommend their favourite books, genres and authors with like-minded peers. A child/tween/teen book club may be purely for recreational reading or it may have a specific goal, such as to engage reluctant readers, extend gifted and talented students, encourage reading amongst ESL students or help young people in their reading transition from primary to high school. My own Year Six Girl Zone Book Club (for girls and a significant woman in their lives) is for this purpose. Book clubs build literary knowledge and skills and they also create memories and positive reading experiences.

The essentials

A designated meeting space. In the past I have rotated meetings through homes, but the emphasis can become the home itself, rather than the reading! Peers will want to explore each other's rooms and adults want to exchange tips for keeping that houseplant alive, which loses the focus. Some families can find it stressful to entertain and cater when it is their turn to host.

With my own book club I have well and truly gone back to 'we meet in the school library twice per term at 6.30pm'. This established routine and known location seems to take away one of the barriers to maintaining the book club.

Members. Clearly you can't have a book club of one, no matter how specific your reading tastes are. A book club is all about reading being a social and shared experience. We co-create meaning from books as we read together and listen to the opinions and thoughts of others. I do highly recommend book clubs with members of a similar age, reading level or interest such as a Harry Potter book club (reading books by J. K. Rowling and then books in a similar style) or a food-themed book club, where young members share favourite recipes, recipe books and food-themed novels. The best way to gather book club members is to clearly advertise your book club, either at school if you're a teacher wanting to start a book club, or via a customer database if you work at a bookstore, or among peers and family friends if you are a parent hoping to start one for your children.

Books to read and ponder. A book club is not a book club without books. You have a few options here.

- Read the same book and discuss it as a group.
- Read different books based around a theme or by the same author and compare and contrast and share titles at your meeting.
- Bring along whichever books you are reading to recommend and share with your peers.
- Put together a collection of books to be read over the year and share these among members, to be read at their leisure.
- Consider a 'first reader' book club if you are in a school library. All newly ordered books go first to book club members who read and review them.

In my Year Six Girl Zone Book Club we read two books and meet twice per term. I choose two to five books to 'book talk' about each meeting and we vote on which books we will read as a group. Except when I decide that book club is not a democracy and I INSIST that all members read a particular book because it is SO GOOD and I want them to read it and agree with me on how great it is. Occasionally this strategy has backfired so I try to stick with the democratic process.

Some literary guidance. For each Girl Zone Book Club I prepare a list of questions based on the book we have just read. These are a guide only and not all have to be answered. I create these questions on sticky notes as I read the book myself and I often also consult any teachers' notes (found online) for further ideas. For me these questions should be open-ended and invite discussion, debate and deep thinking. This is not a comprehension test for an English class; this is mature discussion about literature and should help members to develop their own language around books. I like my questions to guide members to think about how the book connects with their own experience – maybe they see their life reflected in the pages or maybe they feel the book helped them to develop empathy or understanding of a particular topic.

If teachers' notes, author interviews or reviews can be found, I will often send these to book club members before a meeting or print copies for the meeting. I usually find that this 'support material' greatly extends the discussion of a book.

A format for meetings. It's really important to think this through properly. What are your aims? Who is the book club for? You may decide that you want formal and in-depth discussion at your meetings or you may prefer casual chats and an informal vibe. My format is always the same – each person brings a small plate of food to share and I provide tea and coffee. We start with some food and drinks before we move into our discussion time. My book club has between twenty to forty attendees each meeting so we split into groups of about six. For about half an hour each group discusses the books using the prepared literary questions as a guide, and then reports back to the main group and we chat as a whole. I then talk about title choices for our next read, we vote, chat, eat some more and go home for a bit of bedtime reading.

Some years I have included a hands-on activity as part of the meeting, especially when a book has lent itself naturally to this.

I like to allow ten to fifteen minutes towards the end of the meeting for students to share other books they have enjoyed. I ask them to bring the book along to the meeting as well as a summary of the story and two reasons why they are recommending it.

A code of conduct. This helps to keep members on track and if you are a teacher running a book club it helps to put responsibility into the hands of the students, allowing you to be more a facilitator than teacher. Book club meetings are different to teaching an English lesson and you don't want to be standing up the front running things. At the first meeting of the year I always explain the way an adult book club works to the students. We discuss listening to each other, respecting the opinions of others and ensuring there is a balance of students and adults talking and sharing with the group. I also talk about expectations between book club meetings – that everyone will make a concerted effort to read the book in the set time-frame but that you are still very welcome to come along even if you have not finished it. Setting up a code of conduct adds to the feeling of ownership for all members.

The extras. I have been running book clubs for many years now and mostly I keep the format simple, but each year I always organise an end-of-year outing for the members. We visit a local independent bookstore where the owner gives a talk, over wine (and juice!) and cheese, about her favourite books for the age group, plus some for the adults in the audience. We then shop for Christmas presents or holiday reading material, then wander to a local restaurant for a shared meal.

Some years I have been fortunate to be able to invite an author to book club. A few years ago Kate DiCamillo happened to be in Brisbane and her publisher offered to bring her along to our meeting as we were reading her wonderful novel *Raymie Nightingale*. After I picked my jaw up off the ground at being offered a visit from one of the celebrities of children's literature, I tried to write a sensible 'thank you and YES' email reply with not too many over-excited exclamation marks. Kate DiCamillo was everything I imagined: delightful, funny, humble, warm (so warm!), kind and so very interesting. Her book club visit remains a career highlight for me. Visits of this ilk are not a regular occurrence but every so often an author comes to talk to the book club and it always adds a level of excitement and wonder to the event.

HOW TO HOST AN AUTHOR OR ILLUSTRATOR VISIT

If you follow these tips you'll ensure that when an author or illustrator leaves your school you will have inspired students and staff who are ready to continue some deep and meaningful work. Plus a speaker who walks away telling others about the amazing kids they met and the dedicated educators who go above and beyond to ignite a passion for story in their students.

- Seek funding from your school P&C or other source by writing or speaking about the many benefits of author or illustrator visits as outlined in pages 99–102.
- Consult with your local speakers agency about the best author or illustrator for your school and whether the format will be a talk or workshop.
- Gather and read many or all of the author's or illustrator's books before their visit and ensure students and staff have read them too. There is very little point in an author or illustrator visit if the students and staff have no idea at all who the speaker is as the entire session is merely spent getting to know them rather than deeply engaging with their work.
- Complete some work ahead of the visit. For example classes may explore the style and medium that an illustrator uses and create their own pictures using these techniques or they may write compositions based on the text. Most publisher websites will have teaching ideas for particular titles and some will even have extensive curriculum-related teaching notes which have been specifically created for schools.
- Discuss with students what the author may talk about. Brainstorm some rich questions and talk about manners – is it polite or helpful to ask someone how much they earn, how old they are or why they have a bald head? Discuss also the difference

between a question and a comment – does the speaker really need to know that you had a banana smoothie for breakfast and the quinoa flakes your mum added made your mouth feel gluggy? (Yes, that was an actual comment I heard once at a literature festival.)

- Create posters or banners to showcase student work and welcome authors or illustrators to the school community.
- Distribute the timetable of the day's proceedings to the school community and to the speaker so they are aware of which age groups they are talking to and how many students will be in each group.
- Organise a local bookseller to sell books on the day and preferably send home an order form in the week before the visit.
- Organise students to introduce the speaker and welcome them, and students to thank them at the conclusion of the talk. We often ask student leaders to take notes throughout the workshop and at the end share their thoughts on what the class might take away from the visit.
- Check dietary requirements and plan meal breaks and a time to sign books if needed.
- Have your camera or phone on hand to take photographs of the speaker. I use these for writing about the event in the school newsletter or on social media, with permission.

ENDNOTES

Chapter 1

1. Smith, L. & Gasser, M. (2005), 'The development of embodied cognition: six lessons from babies', *Artificial Life*, 11, pp. 13–29.

2. Noble, C., Cameron-Faulkner, T. & Lieven, E. (2018), 'Keeping it simple: the grammatical properties of shared book reading', *Journal of Child Language*, 45(3), pp. 753–766. Retrieved from: doi:10.1017/S0305000917000447

Hoff-Ginsberg, E. (1991), 'Mother-child conversation in different social classes and communicative settings', *Child Development*, 62(4), pp. 782–796. Retrieved from: https://doi.org/10.1111/j.1467-8624.1991.tb01569.x

3. Fletcher, K. L. & Reese, E. (2005), 'Picture book reading with young children: a conceptual framework', *Developmental Review*, 25(1), pp. 64–103. Retrieved from: http://dx.doi.org/10.1016/j.dr. 2004.08.009

4. Flewitt, R., Kucirkova, N. & Messer, D. (2014), 'Touching the virtual, touching the real: iPads and enabling literacy for students experiencing disability', *Australian Journal of Language and Literacy*, 37(2), pp. 107–116.

5. *ibid.* Smith, L. & Gasser, M. (2005).

6. Lee, B. (2017), 'Facilitating reading habits and creating peer culture in shared book reading: an exploratory case study in a toddler classroom', *Early Childhood Education Journal*, 45(4), pp. 521–527. Retrieved from: doi:10.1007/s10643-016-0782-1

7. *ibid.* Lee, B. (2017).

8. Cuskelly, J. (2011), 'A case study using Kodály principles in a language immersion setting', *Australian Kodály Journal*, pp. 24–27.

9. Flint, T. K. & Adams, M. S. (2018), '"It's like playing, but learning": supporting early literacy through responsive play with wordless picture books', *Language Arts*, 96(1), pp. 21–35. Retrieved from: https://gateway.library.qut.edu.au/login?url=https://search-proquest-com.ezp01.library.qut.edu.au/docview/2102833423?accountid=13380

Flint, T. K. (2018), 'Responsive play: creating transformative classroom spaces through play as reader response', *Journal of Early Childhood Literacy*. Retrieved from: doi.org/10.1177/1468798418763991

Evans, J. (2012), '"This is me": developing literacy and a sense of self through play, talk, and stories', *Education 3–13: International Journal of Primary, Elementary and Early Years Education*, 40(3), pp. 315–331.

Mantei, J. & Kervin, L. (2015), 'Examining the interpretations children share from their reading of an almost wordless picture book during independent reading time', *Australian Journal of Language and Literacy*, 38(3), pp. 183–192.

Chapter 2

1. Guthrie, J. T., Hoa, A. L. W., Wigfield, A., Tonks, S. M., Humenick, N. M. & Littles, E. (2007), 'Reading motivation and reading comprehension growth in the later elementary years', *Contemporary Educational Psychology*, 32(3), pp. 282–313. Retrieved from: http://dx.doi.org/10.1016/j.cedpsych.2006.05.004

Lysenko, L. & Abrami, P. (2014), 'Promoting reading comprehension with the use of technology', *Computers & Education*, 75, pp. 162–172. Retrieved from: doi:10.1016/j.compedu.2014.01.010

Shanahan, T. (2006), 'Relations among oral language, reading, and writing development', in C. MacArthur, S. Graham & J. Fitzgerald (Eds.), *Handbook of Writing Research*, Guildford Press, New York, pp. 171–183.

2. Cain, K., Oakhill, J. & Bryant, P. (2004), 'Children's reading comprehension ability: concurrent prediction by working memory, verbal ability, and component skills', *Journal of Educational Psychology*, 96(1), pp. 31–42. Retrieved from: http://dx.doi.org/10.1037/0022-0663.96.1.31

Lysenko, L. & Abrami, P. (2014), 'Promoting reading comprehension with the use of technology', *Computers & Education*, 75, pp. 162–172. Retrieved from: doi:10.1016/j.compedu.2014.01.010

3. Hempenstall, K. (2016), 'Read about it: scientific evidence for effective teaching of reading', CIS Research Report 11, Centre for Independent Studies, Sydney. Retrieved from: https://www.cis.org.au/app/uploads/2016/07/rr11.pdf

Wheldall, K., Wheldall, R., Madelaine, A., Reynolds, M. & Arakelian, S. (2017), 'Further evidence for the efficacy of an evidence-based, small group, literacy intervention program for young struggling readers', *Australian Journal of Learning Difficulties*, 22, pp. 3–13. Retrieved from: doi:10.1080/19404158.2017.1287102

4. Clark, W. & Luckin, R. (2013), 'What the research says – iPads in the classroom', *London Knowledge Lab*. Retrieved from: http://digitalteachingandlearning.files.wordpress.com/2013/03/ iPads-in-the-classroom-report-lkl.pdf

McPake, J., Plowman, L. & Stephen, C. (2013), 'Preschool children creating and communicating with digital technologies in the home', *British Journal of Educational*

Technology, 44(3), pp. 421–431. Retrieved from: http://dx.doi.org/10.1111/j.1467-8535.2012.01323.x

Melhuish, K. & Falloon, G. (2010), 'Looking to the future: M-learning with the iPad. Computers in New Zealand', *Schools: Learning, Leading, Technology*, 22(3), pp. 1–16.

5. Cheung, A. & Slavin, R. E. (2012), 'How features of educational technology programs affect student reading outcomes: a meta-analysis', *Educational Research Review*, 7(3), pp. 198–215. Retrieved from: http://doi.org/10.1016/j.edurev.2012.05.002

Chapter 3

1. Colegrove, T. (2013), 'Editorial board thoughts: libraries as makerspace?', *Information Technology and Libraries* (online), 32(1), pp. 2–5. Retrieved from: https://search.proquest.com/docview/1356913023?accountid=31918

2. American Library Association (2013), 'A history of making'. Retrieved from: http://americanlibrariesmagazine.org/features/02062013/manufacturing-makerspaces

3. Slatter, D. & Zaana, H. (2013), 'A place to make, hack, and learn: makerspaces in Australian public libraries', *The Australian Library Journal*, 62(4), pp. 272–284. Retrieved from: doi:10.1080/00049670.2013.853335

4. *ibid.* Colegrove, T. (2013).

Chapter 4

1. Freeman, G. (2007), 'Reinventing the library' in Kresh, D. (Ed.), *The Whole Digital Library Handbook*, American Library Association, Chicago, pp. 370–374.

2. Lackney, J. (2015), '33 principles of educational design', *The National Clearinghouse for Educational Facilities*. Retrieved from: http://schoolstudio.typepad.com/school_design_studio/33-educational-design-pri.html

3. Groundwater-Smith, S. (2004), 'Transforming learning: transforming places and space for learning', CEFPI Conference: Faculty design and learning: has the paradigm changed?, Conservatorium of Music, Sydney.

Chapter 5

1. Horbec, D. (2012), 'The link between reading and academic success', *English in Australia*, 47(2), pp. 58–67.

Hiebert, E. H., Wilson, K. M. & Trainin, G. (2010), 'Are students really reading in independent reading contexts? An examination of comprehension-based silent reading rate', in E. H. Hiebert & D. R. Reutzel (Eds.), *Revisiting Silent Reading: new directions for teachers and researchers*, International Reading Association, Newark, DE, pp. 151–167.

Larson, Lotta C. (2015), 'E-Books and audiobooks: extending the digital reading experience', *The Reading Teacher*, 69(2), pp. 169–177.

Lyengar, S. & Ball, D. (2007), *To Read or Not to Read: a question of national consequence*, National Endowment for the Arts, Washington, DC.

2. *ibid.* Horbec, D. (2012).

3. Lysenko, L. & Abrami, P. (2014), 'Promoting reading comprehension with the use of technology', *Computers & Education*, 75, pp. 162–172. Retrieved from: doi:10.1016/j.compedu.2014.01.010

Shanahan, T. (2006), 'Relations among oral language, reading, and writing development', in C. MacArthur, S. Graham, & J. Fitzgerald (Eds.), *Handbook of Writing Research*, Guildford Press, New York, pp. 171–183.

Chapter 6

1. *Learning Difficulties Australia* – https://www.ldaustralia.org/

2. Sousa, D. (2014), *How the Brain Learns to Read*, Sage Publications, US, p. 5.

3. SPELD QLD – https://www.speld.org.au/dyslexia

4. SPELD QLD – https://www.speld.org.au/auditory-processing-disorder

5. Centre for Youth Literature (2009), *Keeping Young Australian's Reading* report, State Library of Victoria.

6. Newman, N. (2017), 'What is middle-grade fiction and should you write it?', Australian Writers' Centre's blog. Retrieved from: https://www.writerscentre.com.au/blog/what-is-middle-grade-fiction/

Chapter 7

1. Moynihan, K. E. (2009), 'Local authors in the classroom: bringing readers and writers together', *The English Journal*, 98(3), pp. 34–38.

2. DeFauw, D. L. (2018), 'One school's yearlong collaboration with a children's book author', *The Reading Teacher*, 72(3), pp. 355–367. Retrieved from: https://doi.org/10.1002/trtr.1726

Chapter 9

1. Kalantzis, M., Cope, B., Chan, E. & Dalley-Trim, L. (2016), *Literacies*, Cambridge University Press, Port Melbourne, Australia.

Pahl, K. & Rowsell, J. (2005), *Literacy and Education: understanding the new literacy studies in the classroom*, Paul Chapman Publishing, London.

Bock, M., Pachler, N. & Kress, G. (2013), *Multimodality and Social Semiosis Communication, Meaning-making and Learning in the work of Gunther Kress*, Routledge, New York.

2. Larson, Lotta C. (2015), 'E-Books and audiobooks: extending the digital reading experience', *The Reading Teacher*, 69(2), pp. 169–177.

Moyer, J. (2011), '"Teens today don't read books anymore": a study of differences in interest and comprehension in multiple modalities', in *Proceedings of the 2011 iConference*, pp. 815–816. Retrieved from: https://doi.org/10.1145/1940761.1940918

Lysenko, L. & Abrami, P. (2014), 'Promoting reading comprehension with the use of technology', *Computers & Education*, 75, pp. 162–172. Retrieved from: doi:10.1016/j.compedu.2014.01.010

3. Grover, S. & Hannegan, L. D. (2012), *Listening to Learn: audiobooks supporting literacy*, American Library Association, Chicago, IL.

4. Gander, L. (2013), 'Audiobooks: the greatest asset in the library', *Library Media Connection*, 31(4), p. 48.

Chapter 10

1. Lopatovska, I., Carcamo, T., Dease, N., Jonas, E., Kot, S., Pamperien, G. & Yalcin, K. (2017), 'Not just a pretty picture part two: testing a visual literacy program for young children', *Journal of Documentation*, 74(3), pp. 588–607.

Hattwig, D., Burgess, J., Bussert, K. & Medaille, A. (2011), 'ACRL visual literacy competency standards for higher education', Association of College & Research Libraries. Retrieved from: www.ala.org/acrl/standards/visualliteracy

2. Lukehart, W. (2011), 'Wordless books: picture perfect', *School Library Journal*, 57(4), pp. 50–54.

Serafini, F. (2014), 'Exploring wordless picture books', *The Reading Teacher*, 68(1), pp. 24–26.

3. Greenhoot, A., Beyer, A. & Curtis, J. (2014), 'More than pretty pictures? How illustrations affect parent-child story reading and children's story recall', *Frontiers in Psychology*, 5.

4. Feathers, K. & Arya, P. (2012), 'The role of illustrations during children's reading', *The Journal of Children's Literature*, 38(1), pp. 36–43.

Chapter 12

1. Jha, A. P., Krompinger, J. & Baime, M. J. (2007), 'Mindfulness training modifies subsystems of attention', *Cogn Affect Behav Neurosci*, 7(2), pp. 109–119. Retrieved from: doi:10.3758/CABN.7.2.109

Zylowska, L., Ackerman, D. L., Yang, M. H., Futrell, J. L., Horton, N. L., Hale, T. S., et al. (2008), 'Mindfulness meditation training in adults and adolescents with ADHD: a feasibility study', *J. Atten. Disord*, 11(6), pp. 737–746. Retrieved from: doi: 10.1177/1087054707308502

Hodgins, H. S. & Adair, K. C. (2010), 'Attentional processes and meditation', *Conscious Cogn.*, 19(4), pp. 872–878. Retrieved from: doi:10.1016/j.concog.2010.04.002

Tarrasch, R., Berman, Z. & Friedmann, N. (2016), 'Mindful reading: mindfulness meditation helps keep readers with dyslexia or ADHD on the lexical track', *Frontiers in Psychology*, 7(May), p. 578. Retrieved from: doi:10.3389/fpsyg.2016.00578

2. *ibid.* Tarrasch, R., Berman, Z. & Friedmann, N. (2016).

3. ACARA (2012), 'The Australian Curriculum', Sydney.

Chapter 13

1. Australia Council for the Arts (2007), *Protocols for Producing Indigenous Australian Writing.* Retrieved from: http://www.australiacouncil.gov.au/symphony/extension/richtext_redactor/getfile/?name=fc8a5cc73467cb405e8943ae14975da7.pdf

Harrison, J. interviewed by Adeney, A. (2017), 'Question your motives', Writers Victoria website. Retrieved from: https://writersvictoria.org.au/writing-life/on-writing/question-your-motives

2. Heiss, A. (2014), 'Writing Indigenous characters: an interview', blog post. Retrieved from: https://anitaheiss.wordpress.com/2014/11/14/writing-indigenous-characters-an-interview/

3. BlackWords – https://www.austlit.edu.au/specialistDatasets/BlackWords

Atkinson, M. (2017), 'Read, listen, understand: why non-Indigenous Australians should read First Nations writing', *The Conversation*. Retrieved from: http://theconversation.com/read-listen-understand-why-non-indigenous-australians-should-read-first-nations-writing-78925

Tan, M. (2016), 'Indigenous writer Bruce Pascoe: we need novels that are true to the land', *The Guardian*. Retrieved from: https://www.theguardian.com/books/2016/feb/18/indigenous-writer-bruce-pascoe-on-why-australias-literary-giants-have-failed

Sheldon-Collins, D. (2014), '"Getting it right": Anita Heiss on Indigenous characters', The Wheeler Centre website. Retrieved from: https://www.wheelercentre.com/notes/221927959a6b

4. Birch, T. interviewed by McLaren, M. (2015), 'Approaching Indigenous characters and culture', Writers Victoria website. Retrieved from: https://writersvictoria.org.au/writing-life/on-writing/approaching-indigenous-characters-and-culture

Roger, M. (2016), 'Taking control of our stories', Writers Victoria website. Retrieved from: https://writersvictoria.org.au/writing-life/featured-writers/taking-control

5. Heiss, A. (2016), '20 Reasons you should read blak', blog post. Retrieved from: https://anitaheiss.wordpress.com/2016/02/21/20-reasons-you-should-read-blak/

Heiss, A. (2011), 'Black Book Challenge', blog post. Retrieved from: https://anitaheiss.wordpress.com/2011/04/23/anitas-black-book-challenge-bbc/

CONTRIBUTOR BIOGRAPHIES

Kathryn Apel is a born-and-bred farm girl who's scared of cows. *Too Many Friends* is Kathryn's fifth book and third verse novel, following the release of *On Track* (2015) and *Bully on the Bus* (2014) to much acclaim. Kathryn loves pumping poetry because she can flex her muscles across other genres, to bend (and break) writing rules. A trained teacher and literacy coach, Kathryn now shares her passion for words at schools and festivals. katswhiskers.wordpress.com

Stephen Axelsen has been a children's book illustrator and author for time immemorial, specialising in humour and fantasy. He has a long history of making 'sequential art', in the shape of cartoon series for *The School Magazine* and graphic novels. He is best known to a close circle of family and friends.

Des Crump's Gamilaroi family is from the Goondiwindi district. He has a teaching background working in primary teaching, secondary guidance and curriculum policy prior to establishing his own consultancy where he continues to work in Aboriginal education but also with Aboriginal and Torres Strait Islander languages. Des is the Coordinator of the Indigenous Languages Project at the State Library of Queensland. Qualifications include: Masters of Indigenous Languages Education; Masters of Education (Guidance and Counselling); Bachelor of Education; Graduate Diploma in Aboriginal Education; Graduate Diploma Education Studies (Careers); Diploma of Teaching (Primary).

Tracey Hand is the co-founder of Optimise Learning and an experienced educator who is passionate about assisting students to engage in learning and achieve to their full potential. Tracey has extensive classroom experience and has held a variety of roles within school settings in Australia and Singapore. Tracey is a qualified Reading Recovery teacher, a QSA-trained Preparatory Facilitator and a QSA-trained Curriculum Assessment and Reporting Framework Facilitator. A skilled presenter, Tracey has held workshops for a number of organisations.

Jacqueline Harvey is one of Australia's most popular authors for children, having sold over a million copies of her Alice-Miranda and Clementine Rose series in Australia alone. Her new spy series, Kensy and Max, is already thrilling young readers with drama, action and loads of fun. She has received numerous shortlistings and awards while her picture book, *The Sound of the Sea,* was a CBCA Honour Book. A highly experienced teacher and presenter, Jacqueline has delivered thousands of talks and workshops at schools and festivals around the world.

Shona Innes is a clinical and forensic psychologist with many years of experience helping others. As well as individualising psychological interventions for a wide range of people and behaviours, Shona has advised organisations, big and small, about promoting better mental health, safe behaviours and the right kind of ways to manage and support others with problem behaviour or in troubling situations. Her children's book series, The Big Hug Books, grew out of individual therapy sessions with children and their families.

Will Kostakis is a writer of all things, from celebrity news stories that score cease and desist letters, to tweets for professional wrestlers. He's best known for his award-winning YA novels, *The Sidekicks* and *The First Third*. His first fantasy novel series, *Monuments*, begins in 2019.

Joy Lawn writes the YA literature column for the *Weekend Australian* and interviews authors for *Magpies* magazine. She judges the Prime Minister's Literary Awards, has an MA in Children's Literature and Literacy and loves facilitating sessions at the Sydney and Brisbane Writers' Festivals. Joy promotes Australian literature here and overseas.

Georgina Manning is the director of Wellbeing for Kids and a counsellor and psychotherapist. Georgina runs regular parent seminars in schools, training for school staff and is a national speaker for wellbeing events. Georgina has created the 'Peaceful Kids' and 'Peaceful Parents' Mindfulness and Positive Psychology programs and holds training for school staff and mental health professionals across many states in Australia.

Sophie Masson is the award-winning, internationally published author of more than 60 books for children, young adults and adults. In 2018, she successfully completed a Creative Practice PhD at the University of New England (NSW), which included a novel, *The Ghost Squad*, with accompanying exegesis. She is a founding partner in and co-director of Christmas Press, an acclaimed boutique children's publishing house specialising in beautiful illustrated books for children, from picture books featuring retellings of traditional tales by well-known authors, as well as anthologies, novels, plays and poetry, and books featuring both established and emerging writers and illustrators.

Kelly McDonough is a registered nurse turned full-time mother of five. She shares her passion for beautiful and realistic home interiors through her blog *The Styling Mama*, with a focus on children's spaces. She writes for a number of online and print publications, sharing parenting advice, tricks and DIY hacks.

Belinda Murrell is a bestselling, internationally published children's author with a history of writing in her family that spans over 200 years. Her previous titles include four picture books, her fantasy adventure series The Sun Sword trilogy and her seven time-slip adventures, *The Locket of Dreams, The Ruby Talisman, The Ivory Rose, The Forgotten Pearl, The River Charm, The Sequin Star,* and *The Lost Sapphire.* These books have been recognised by various awards. For younger readers (aged six to nine) Belinda has the popular Lulu Bell series about friends, family and animal adventures in a vet hospital, and a middle-grade series called Pippa's Island.

Dr Lyndal O'Gorman is a senior lecturer in the School of Early Childhood and Inclusive Education at Queensland University of Technology. Lyndal has taught in primary schools in Brisbane and Far North Queensland. Her current teaching and research at QUT explores early childhood and primary arts education, education for sustainability, play pedagogies, interdisciplinary learning and teaching, and early childhood leadership. She is particularly interested in the intersection of the arts and education for sustainability.

Natalie Jane Prior is the author of numerous books for children and young adults. Her work includes the classic picture book *The Paw* and its sequels (illustrated by Terry Denton), and the internationally successful fantasy series Lily Quench, which has well over half a million copies in print, and which was broadcast on BBC Radio in

2006. Natalie's books have won the Aurealis Award (for fantasy and science fiction), the Davitt Awards (for crime writing), and have been Honour, shortlisted and Notable Books in the CBCA Awards.

Allison Rushby is the internationally published author of over twenty novels. Her latest middle-grade novels are *The Mulberry Tree* and the Davitt Award-winning *The Turnkey*. A sequel to *The Turnkey*, titled *The Seven Keys*, will be published in 2019. www.allisonrushby.com

Award-winning author **Pamela Rushby** has worked in advertising, as a preschool teacher, and a freelance writer. She was a writer and producer of educational television, audio and multimedia for the Queensland Department of Education for sixteen years, and now freelances in children's and young adult fiction and non-fiction; scriptwriting; and multimedia writing/designing. Pamela Rushby has over 200 books to her credit and is passionately interested in children's books and television, ancient history and Middle Eastern food.

Emma Schafer is an early childhood educator who has taught across Australia. She has taught in a variety of before school settings using a number of curriculums including the International Baccalaureate, the Early Years Learning Framework and the Queensland Kindergarten Learning Guidelines. Emma has also completed her Master of Education in Leadership and Management.

R. A. Spratt is a bestselling author and television writer. She is known for the Nanny Piggins, Friday Barnes and Peski Kids series of books. R. A. Spratt has written for dozens of different television shows. In recent years she has specialised mainly in children's animation, but she has also had extensive experience writing jokes, sketch comedy and political satire.

Allison Tait (A. L. Tait) is the internationally published bestselling author of middle-grade adventure series The Mapmaker Chronicles and the Ateban Cipher. A multi-genre writer and accomplished speaker, Allison also co-hosts the top-rating *So You Want To Be A Writer* podcast and teaches creative writing for adults and kids at the Australian Writers' Centre.

Jennifer Teh is the founding director of Hush Little Baby Early Childhood Music Classes. Jen has taught everything from primary, high school and university music, directed choirs, taught private singing lessons, presented workshops, written papers for national and international conferences and symposia in music education and carved out a career as a professional live and studio singer. Jen's passion lies in early childhood music education, and this is supported by a huge body of research around the positive benefits of sharing music with infants and children.

Joe Visser has been reviewing books at bookboy.com.au since he was twelve and, in 2018, aged fourteen, was the first teen member of the #LoveOzYA committee. Now fifteen, Joe blogs less regularly, focusing instead on his schoolwork and burgeoning career as a singer/songwriter (you can hear his music on his website). But he continues to read voraciously.

Michelle Witheyman-Crump is an author and teacher librarian. Her first book, *Original Girl*, was the story of her Indigenous daughter. As the eldest child of three, with parents who were foster carers, Michelle grew up with many children from various cultural backgrounds sharing her home, and many of these experiences have shaped her as a person and as an author. She is a teacher librarian in Ipswich, editor for the Ipswich District Teacher Librarian Book Week Publication and on the committee of the Story Arts Festival Ipswich.

ACKNOWLEDGEMENTS

The very first acknowledgement and thanks must go to my children, referred to in this book and online as ChickPea and PudStar; thank you for being strong and sassy and loving me endlessly. Thanks also to my immediate and extended family, particularly my parents Robyn and Geoff Dean and siblings Amber and Jeremy, who have dealt with their own grief and trauma while supporting the girls and me through ours. Those of you who know me through my blog will know that my husband, to whom this book is dedicated (along with my brother), passed away in 2017. Family, friends, a wonderful school/work community and books have sustained us through these past few years. I always knew that books had the power to offer support through tragic circumstances but now, from personal experience, I can say that books have been a necessary and life-affirming part of our post-traumatic growth. I am endlessly grateful that my literary community, both online and offline, has reached out in so many ways to ease my load and gift me the right books at the right time. Understandably, the acknowledgements section of *Raising Readers* is entirely longer than it should be, much like most Academy Award speeches.

There are many people who need to be thanked and without them this book would not exist. I am so grateful that Dan was with us to see the contract on this book signed and read the first two or three chapters. He was so immensely supportive of my work and, as an avid reader himself, he well understood the power of books in the lives of children and adults. Through his years of crippling chronic pain, Dan would often escape into books of all kinds and he awaited every new Ranger's Apprentice and Brotherband book by John Flanagan with the patience (impatience) of a child waiting for Christmas. Dan introduced my father and brother to these series and while none of them were in the target age audience by a long shot, they all become obsessed with them, often texting me late at night to get the next from my school library. Quality books are ageless, and now my brother Jeremy has introduced our niece to them. It is heartbreaking and soul-soothing in equal measure to know that Dan was the 'one' who introduced Ranger's Apprentice to my family.

The remainder of this book was written after Dan's death and the people listed below held the girls and I afloat and shone a light in our darkness while I wrote. They entertained my children, did my washing, contributed their time in editing the entire tome many times over and in offering written advice, most especially Trish Buckley (#alwaystrish). This is not a list of people who have personally helped us over the last two years – that would require a much longer acknowledgements altogether!

Thanks to:

Jackie Child
Catherine Bryant
Pauline Mcleod
Alex Boyd
Fiona Stager
Mel Kroeger/Joanne Curry/Kym Potts (you exist as a unit and are listed as such)
Herb/Doug/Steve
Ken and Debbie Acworth
Renee and Trent Smith
Sam Lloyd and Stuart Mutzig
Allison Burton Jones
Jo Mitchell

Sam Doig
Jenny Stubbs
Heather Marshall
Tracey Jeanes Fraser
Jen Golden
Beth Miller
Zahra Jeanes Fraser
Justine Frkovic
The junior school staff of St Aidan's Anglican Girls' School
Jessica Rudd
Rebecca Sparrow
Samantha Wheeler
Riverbend Books
Avid Reader
Melissa Keil.

Heartfelt thanks to each of the contributors to this book, whose names and biographies can be found on pages 238–243; to publish your words among my own is a privilege.

The final thanks goes to Kristina Schulz for her commitment to this book and for making it happen in the first place. She came to check me out at what turned out to be the worst public speaking event I have ever done and yet she still sidled up to me afterwards and said, 'I think you have a book in you.' She then gently hounded me about said book for quite some time and ignored my protests that I reviewed books, not wrote them. Thank you to the entire team at UQP, particularly Cathy Vallance, Jody Lee and Jo Hunt. UQP has long been one of my top three Australian publishers and I am honoured to now reside among your list of published authors.